EFFECTIVE WRITING
FOR BUSINESS, COLLEGE & LIFE

William R. Stanek

Revised Edition Copyright © 2009 by William R. Stanek. All rights reserved, including the right to reproduce this book, or portions thereof, in any form. No portion of this book may be reproduced or transmitted in any form or by any means without express written permission of the publisher. Printed in the United States of America.

Reagent Press, LLC

Cover design & illustration by William R. Stanek

ISBN-10: 1-57545-245-6

ISBN-13: 978-1-57545-245-6

Microsoft, Windows, Windows XP and Windows Vista are either registered trademarks or trademarks of Microsoft Corporation in the United States and/or other countries. Intel is a registered trademark of Intel Corporation. Other products mentions herein may be the trademarks of their respective owners.

Any characters, names, places and events portrayed in this book are either products of the author's imagination or are used fictitiously. Any resemblance to any actual locale, person or event is entirely coincidental. While every precaution has been taken in production of this book, the publisher assumes no responsibility for errors or omissions, or for damages resulting from the use of the information contained herein.

Table of Contents

PART I: GETTING ORGANIZED 7

CHAPTER 1: BUILDING BLOCKS FOR EFFECTIVE WRITING 9
Managing Expectations 11
Managing Perceptions 12
Managing Strategies 13
Managing Goals 14
Managing Rules 15
Managing Behavior 16

CHAPTER 2: IMPROVING IDEAS: TECHNIQUES TO BETTER ORGANIZE 19
Brainstorming Techniques 20
Freethinking Techniques 22
Storyboarding Techniques 23

CHAPTER 3: EFFECTIVE STRATEGIES FOR PLANNING AND ORGANIZATION 25
Composition Processes 25
Development Processes 31
Pre-Finalization Processes 39
Combining It All 44

CHAPTER 4: TECHNIQUES TO GET STARTED 47
Setting a Schedule 47
Connecting Milestones and Goals 49

CHAPTER 5: TECHNIQUES TO ORGANIZE FOR THE AUDIENCE 53
Defining the Audience 53
Seeing With the Reader's Eyes 55
Gathering Statistics 56
Evaluating Trends 57

CHAPTER 6: ORGANIZING THROUGH STORYBOARDING ... 59
Working with Storyboards ... 59
Developing Structure Using Storyboards ... 62
Developing Content Using Storyboards ... 65
Evaluating Storyboard Organization ... 68

PART I: QUICK REVIEW ... 69

PART II: PAGE DESIGN ... 73

CHAPTER 7: DESIGNING WITH SPACE ... 75
Using Space Effectively ... 75
Sizing Your Paragraphs ... 76
Adding Graphics ... 76

CHAPTER 8: UNDERSTANDING COLOR ... 79
What Does Color Represent? ... 79
Using Color in Presentations ... 80

CHAPTER 9: POWERFUL HEADINGS ... 83
Headings: Best Uses ... 83
Good Headings vs. Bad Headings ... 84

CHAPTER 10: EXPLORING FONTS ... 85
Working with Fonts ... 85
Deciding Which Font to Use ... 86

CHAPTER 11: UNLEASHING PAGE LAYOUT ... 91
How Graphic Designers Use Grids ... 91
Text Components in Page Design ... 92
Graphic Components in Page Design ... 93

PART II: QUICK REVIEW ... 95

PART III: TAPPING INTO THE POWER OF MULTIMEDIA ... 97

CHAPTER 12: MULTIMEDIA BONANZA 99
What is JPEG? 100
What is MPEG? 101
Considerations to Make Before Adding Multimedia 106
Let's Talk Sound 107
Let's Talk Video 112
Let's Talk New Media 115
The Critical Question Of Resources 119

PART III: QUICK REVIEW 121

PART IV: DELIVERING YOUR WORK 123

CHAPTER 13: LAST MINUTE GOTCHAS 125
What to Look For when Proofing 125
Tips for Checking Spelling 129
Tips for Checking Grammar 133
How to Catch Typos Outside Main Text 139
How to Catch Inconsistencies 140
Balancing Perfection with Efficiency and Timeliness 142

PART IV: QUICK REVIEW 145

ABOUT THE AUTHOR 146

WE NEED YOU 146

Part I: Getting Organized

Blockbusters are not written, they are produced. Look at today's hit movies and TV shows. Behind the big scenes, you will find a producer and often a collaborative team. Print and digital mediums are no exception.

Behind the big titles, you will find a team—editors, writers, and designers. All these people help to organize ideas into a finely polished work. They do this by collaborating—organizing their ideas into a common structure through planning, revision, polishing, and evaluation.

Even when creative works are the result of a single person's efforts, the finished product is still a result of planning, revision, polishing, and fretting over the organization of the work. This is true even for creative people who claim never to use outlines. The simple fact is, finely polished works do not spring to the writer's pen, the painter's canvas, or the musician's note sheets.

The best works are the result of effective strategies for thinking, planning, and composing. Helping you create the best work through effective strategies for thinking, planning, and composing is precisely what this section is all about.

You will learn

- Why organization is important
- The building blocks for effective writing
- Techniques to better organize and improve ideas
- Effective strategies for planning and organization
- Techniques to get started

- Techniques to organize for the audience
- Storyboards as an organization tool

Spending a few hours thinking about something that you may spend months, or certainly days, working on makes sense. Getting organized is extremely important, more so when you are working in a new genre, medium or subject area.

Not only will good organization save you time, it will help you produce a better final product. This is true regardless of whether you plan to adapt existing works or create entirely new works.

Chapter 1: Building Blocks for Effective Writing

Think of the creative process as a building process. Try to build the roof of the house before you lay the foundation, and you are going to have serious problems. Pour the concrete for the foundation of the house before you put in the necessary plumbing for water and sewer access, and you are going to spend more money than you bargained for.

You build a house one step at a time. You ensure the house has a strong foundation. Buildings with strong foundations tend to weather the seasons and time. When you are almost done with the frame of the house, you build a roof. Although the roof of the house is the top of the structure, you do not stop there. It takes more than a covered frame to make a house. You hire an electrician to do the wiring and bring back the plumber to finish the plumbing. Afterward, you hang plaster board, add insulation, finish the exterior, add fixtures, and before you know it, you have a house that you can call home.

You build your blockbuster in the same way, one step at a time. The most important step is to stop treating your writing as an article, story, book or report and start treating it as a project—*yeah, that's right, big picture baby!* It's all about thinking large, thinking different, and delivering your best. You are working on a project—a project that follows the rules of any good project and includes much more than simple writing.

Your start on the project is about as glamorous as the water and sewer pipes waiting for the foundation to be poured around them; for just when you are ready to roll back your sleeves and dive into the project with both feet, you may discover you need to conduct research, start planning, or consider the requirements of the project. When you finally flesh out the foundation of the project, you start to build the framework.

The basic components of any writing are the pages that you link together. These pages help you create chapters, articles and columns. Even when you have completed the composing and developing processes, the project still is not finished. You check the structure of the work for flaws. You make sure you have used the right mechanics and format. You examine the fixtures. Once all this is done, you finally have a project worthy of presenting to your colleagues, submitting to your professor, or delivering to your editor.

Try to build the house all at once and you will be overwhelmed. The same is true for any creative process. The way you organize your thoughts can make the difference between a successful project and a failed project. When you are building your blockbuster, you need to manage many things. Both on a level of general organization and a more specific level tailored to the current project. This includes:

- Expectations
- Perceptions
- Strategies
- Goals
- Rules
- Behavior

Managing Expectations

If you mismanage expectations your project will fail. Your expectations and the expectations of your editor, your boss, or your professor may be totally different. Before you begin any project, make sure your expectations and the expectations of those who will review the material mesh. A good way to do this is to ensure that the communications channels are open and used.

Discuss expectations from the beginning of the project. Consider developing a rapid prototype of the project in which you write a partial work geared toward the intended audience and deliver this as a sample. If you develop a rapid prototype of the project, your colleagues, peers or superiors should be the ones to verify that it meets their expectations. If the prototype does not meet their expectations, maybe the prototype was an example of what not to do for this project, or maybe the expectations were unrealistic.

You should also manage your personal expectations for the project. Your expectations play a major role in the success or failure of the project. The following is a list of do's and dont's to help you manage expectations:

- Don't expect the creation and development of the project to flow effortlessly.
- Don't expect first efforts to be perfect.
- Don't expect the completed project to be perfect.
- Do expect to make multiple drafts of the project.
- Do expect to revise, edit, and proof parts of the project.

- Do expect to say the project is "good enough" and that further time spent trying to perfect the project will not be cost- or time-effective.

Managing Perceptions

Your perceptions about the project play a decisive role in whether you will ever finish the project. If you perceive the project as an impossibly large undertaking you may cripple yourself mentally. If you perceive the project as a trivial undertaking you will not produce your best work.

It is best to find a balance in your perceptions about the project. If you are working on an extremely large project, work on the project in manageable pieces. Do not try to combine the composition and development processes. Take them one at a time. Develop the textual part of the project a chapter, page, or word at a time—whatever it takes to pull you through the project—and then develop charts, graphs, and other artwork the project requires.

As you begin to organize your project, keep in mind that writing is very often a team effort. Few writers will be able to handle all aspects of every project on their own.

For this reason, you should have an accurate perception of your abilities and know when it is in the best interest of the project to delegate tasks or to look for additional help. For example, if a project covers yacht racing and you know a great deal about sailing but nothing about yacht racing, enlisting the help of or interviewing someone who has actually raced yachts will help tremendously. Not only will delegating tasks to other team members or obtaining outside expertise help ensure the success of the project, it will also take responsibilities off your shoulders and help you avoid feeling overwhelmed.

Managing Strategies

Could you imagine the task of writing 12,500,000 words, developing thousands of graphic images, and filling 40,000 pages? The thought of having to do this would overwhelm the best of writers. Yet, this is exactly what I've done in the last 20 years of writing.

Now, I didn't start out thinking I would ever write so many words, fill so many pages, or complete so many books. I managed projects one step of time and by thinking of the work in terms that motivated me. Most books I write are about 150,000 words and 500 pages, so it wasn't 149,000 words I had to write, it was 1,000 words completed. It wasn't 475 pages more to go, it was 25 pages down. It wasn't 19 chapters left to write, it was one chapter completed.

How you think about a project will materially affect the outcome. Manage the project in whatever way will motivate you. If one way of thinking about the project is not motivating you, change tactics. Break up difficult sections of the project. Tackle them one piece at a time. Rotate from section to section, working on each piece a little at a time. *Whatever it takes to get the job done.*

As a writer you will often wear many hats. You may have the role of the writer, graphic designer, composer, editor and even publisher. You may want to develop a strategy with these roles in mind. For example, if you are in the role of the writer and have been staring at a blank page for hours, you may want to change roles for a time. Why not create the preliminary art for a particular area of the project? This will give you a chance to work on another area of the project and you can return to writing at a later time with a fresh perspective.

Similarly, if you are working on a mundane but necessary part of the project, such as proofreading, think of a way to make the work more interesting or challenging. Bet yourself that you cannot proof portions of the project in certain amounts of time. And when you succeed, allow yourself a few moments of quiet celebration before you attack the project again.

Do not limit yourself to a few strategies or stick with one strategy when it obviously is not working. Make a list of strategies. If one strategy is not working, switch to a new one. If you do not have a new one, create a new one.

Managing Goals

When you start working on a project, one of the first things you should do is develop goals. Goals are usually developed in the requirements phase of a project. Your goals should take into consideration the complexities and nuances of the project. Goals should be clear and relevant to the problem at hand. You should set major goals relevant to the purpose, scope, and audience of the project. You should also set minor goals or milestones for the stages of the project.

Goals and milestones help you define the project as a series of steps, processes or achievements. One major goal could be to complete the planning phase of the project. Another major goal could be to complete the design of the project. The series of steps or processes necessary to complete the major goals are the minor goals or milestones. Your first milestone will be to start work on the project. Another milestone may be to select and purchase necessary resources.

Managing Rules

You will probably create or be provided rules that pertain specifically to the project. As you start the project, these rules may seem perfectly acceptable. However, as you conduct planning for the project you may find that the choices you've been given aren't the best or that certain rules are too restrictive for your needs.

If these early rules cannot be modified to fit the project, you will have problems. You may encounter delays due to loss of efficiency. The final product may not be what was expected. Or worse, the project could be a dismal failure.

Few rules should ever be considered absolute. Even the best of rules should be interpreted as guidelines that can vary depending on the situation. Rules for a project should be flexible and make sense. A rule that conflicts with something you are trying to do in the project should be reexamined. The rule may be inappropriate for the situation you are trying to apply it to.

That said, professors, editors and bosses do sometimes define rules that cannot be changed. These rules should be thought of as mandated rules.

Before breaking or stretching a mandated rule, you should discuss the rule and your intent with the person who assigned the project. If you are clear of purpose and persuasive, there may be some flexibility in the mandated rule after all.

Otherwise, you will need to modify your project to fit the specified requirements.

Managing Behavior

A project will never get finished if you avoid working on it. Putting off work until something is due is a poor practice. Quitting when things do not go your way or when you seem to have a block is another poor practice.

Even if you are one of those people who thrives on deadlines, plan to work on a project regularly—every day if necessary and possible. You should also plan to work on the project during those times when your thoughts are not flowing. Everyone has bad days and good days. Some days you take more breaks. Some days you work straight through the day and into the night.

You may tend toward other destructive behavior besides avoiding or putting off work. Sometimes writers go to the opposite extreme. They tear things apart impulsively before letting the work cool off so they can look at it objectively. Never edit, revise, or proof material immediately after it is drafted or put in near-final form.

For example, you have just completed the implementation phase of the project. You have been working on the project 16 hours a day for three weeks. You tell yourself if you do some minor tweaking now the project will be finished.

You start correcting minor problems and before you know it, you are changing the project drastically because things do not seem to fit right, or you are cutting Chapter 18. At this point, an alarm should go off in your mind. Take a break for a day or two before going back to the project. Trust me, you will be thankful you did.

> ***Reality Check:*** *When working on a project, you should back it up regularly. I keep a master copy and at least one backup copy of all projects on a USB drive and on my hard drive. I also have my word processor set to make automatic saves of my work every five minutes. You will be thankful for backups if you delete material in the heat of the moment and later regret it. Disk space is cheap compared to your time and ideas.*

Chapter 2: Improving Ideas: Techniques to Better Organize

To improve your ideas, you must think in new ways. You must examine the ordinary through different eyes. You must look at the mundane in a new light. You must examine your ideas in fresh ways.

Tapping into your creativity is not a simple process. People have been trying to figure out how to tap into creativity throughout history. One of the great thinkers on the subject of creativity was Abraham Maslow. Maslow discussed creativity in terms of primary and secondary creativity:

- Secondary creativity is a restrictive creativity—the creativity of adults that is based on the creativity of others.

- Primary creativity is an innocent or original creativity—the creativity of children, which is blocked off by most adults and a part of our subconscious thoughts.

Maslow further said that creativity is not necessarily the trait of those who are geniuses or talented, meaning that the fact that someone is a genius or has certain talents does not mean they are also creative.

Maslow's theories on creativity are very important to help people improve ideas. These theories:

- Suggest that you probably could tap into your creative processes by reaching into your subconscious mind.

- Suggest you should try to think freely without the inhibitions placed upon you by society or age.

- Suggest you should look at your ideas through innocent or unjudging eyes.

Many modern techniques for aiding the creative process come out of this school of thinking, such as the following:

- Brainstorming
- Freethinking
- Storyboarding

Let's examine each of these techniques in turn.

> **Reality Check:** *While techniques to improve ideas are most often used at the beginning of projects, they can and should be used any time you want to try to improve your ideas. You may find these techniques especially useful at key stages in project development. For example, if you are considering what type of graphs to include in the project, why not try brainstorming, freethinking or storyboarding as a way of ensuring you make the best choices?*

Brainstorming Techniques

Brainstorming was originally developed as a group problem-solving technique. The members of a brainstorming group were given a set of strict rules governing their behavior. These rules were designed to break down communication barriers.

They did this by protecting the egos of the group members and promoting the need to be a productive member of the group.

The following are the basic rules of brainstorming:

- No evaluation of any ideas put forth are permitted.
- Realize that the ideas put forth are simply ideas and not solutions.
- Free your mind by first thinking of the wildest answers to the problem.
- Throw out as many ideas as you can—every idea that comes into your mind.
- Build on the ideas of other group members.
- When the ideas get more difficult to think of do not stop, the best ideas are just ahead.

Similar concepts can be applied to single-person efforts. Brainstorming can boost your creativity tremendously. If you brainstorm, you will tend to be less critical of your work. Eventually, you will also tend to naturally think of more than one approach to solving a problem.

For one-person brainstorming efforts, the following are good techniques to follow:

- Identify the problem, purpose, audience, or subject you want to brainstorm.
- Write this down in the middle of a large piece of paper and circle it.
- Write down all the ideas that come to your mind concerning the topic and circle them.
- Do not stop until you have filled the page.

- Look for patterns or repeated ideas.
- Use these ideas to develop further ideas or to develop solutions.

Freethinking Techniques

Freethinking is another effective technique to boost your creativity. When you freethink, you begin by telling yourself, "I will think something!" You think about a topic for a set period, recording your thoughts. Another term for freethinking is freewriting. The latter term tends to be more restrictive than necessary because the form of your freethinking efforts does not have to be written.

When you freethink, you should record your thoughts in the way that makes you most comfortable—on paper, a tape recorder, or on a computer. You should also select a period for freethinking you are comfortable with. Ten minutes may be right for some people. Others may prefer longer or shorter periods. After a freethinking session, you review what you recorded and note the ideas you liked.

Often, several freethinking sessions are necessary to get the best ideas. For most people, two or three successive freethinking sessions may be enough to help generate their best material. Others may wish to try a series of freethinking sessions over a period of several days. The key is to find the freethinking method that works best for you and use it.

Storyboarding Techniques

Storyboards are a high-power approach to creative thinking. They are particularly useful for long projects because of the way they help you structure ideas visually. When you storyboard, you represent each section of the presentation in miniature form on a planning sheet and create a mockup of the project.

The storyboard not only serves as an outline for the presentation, it lets you visualize the project in a way you otherwise would not be able to. At a glance, you can see the work from start to finish and this is extremely important in the way you conceptualize the project.

The project is no longer a mysterious tangle of words or pages that you have to string together. It has a logical order from beginning to end. Often, being able to see to the end of a complex project is 75 percent of the battle. Techniques used in storyboarding will be discussed in depth later.

Chapter 3: Effective Strategies for Planning and Organization

Collaborative writing is ideally a team effort, with each member of the team working in an area of the project in which they specialize. In the real world, things don't always turn out ideally. Very often the writer is alone and must wear many hats. They must be the writer, artist, musician, editor, researcher, and whatever else is necessary to get the job done. They are the project's manager, and they alone must see the project to the end.

The tasks involved in each of these roles can be broken down into three broad categories.

- Composition processes
- Development processes
- Pre-finalization processes

While composition and pre-finalization processes are an essential part of every creative project, development processes are primarily for use with projects that require multimedia or are designed for digital media. When I refer to digital media, I am referring to CD ROM publishing, the Internet, e-books and other electronic formats.

Composition Processes

The processes involved in creating original material can be broadly defined as *composition processes*. In the role of the writer, artist, or musician, you create new material or adapt existing material.

Even if you work directly with writers, artists, or musicians or purchase existing material, at some point you must evaluate the work within the scope of the composition processes.

Contrary to popular opinion, the creative process is not some mythical beast that you must hunt down. You may discover many ways to compose a work and many ways to get to the final product. This is true no matter the form of the creation, but generally composition processes include seven activities.

- Planning
- Researching
- Composing
- Evaluating
- Revising
- Editing
- Proofing

Dispelling Myths

Before discussing these activities, let's dispel some myths about the creative process. Just because there are seven activities does not mean you have to perform them all. You will use more of these activities when you are working in new mediums. When you are writing about a new subject area you will tend to use more of the activities than if you were writing about a subject with which you were very familiar. If you are writing for an audience you have never before written for, you may want to follow the seven steps of the composing process carefully. The same holds true when you are creating a new type of work, such as switching from fiction to nonfiction titles.

You can perform the activities in any order you choose and you do not have to finish one activity before you start another. Sometimes you create an outline for the work. Sometimes you create the work first, pause to think about the structure, and then plan how to make the work better. Sometimes you tackle the work a section at a time, planning in spurts. Sometimes you are so familiar with your subject or the medium you are working in that planning is a natural part of your thought process.

Although planning is an important stage of the creative process, it is not the most important stage. This is contrary to the traditional school of thought that stressed planning and specifically advised writers to create an outline for everything they wrote. Whether you create an outline or do not create an outline is not going to materially influence the quality of your work. Research into the creative process has shown that what matters most is how you organize your thoughts and the work.

Planning

When you plan, choose the way in which you are going to organize the work. You do this by drawing on experiences or thinking of new ways to create and organize material. Planning also means thinking about the strategies you are going to use to create the work. It involves analyzing the purpose, scope, and audience for the work. The purpose of the work is the reason you are creating the work or adding to an existing work. Are you adding artwork to accent or clarify the story line? Are you adding music to heighten the mood?

The scope of the work defines what the work encompasses or the extent of the work. Scope can sometimes be defined in terms of focus and size. Is the work broadly or narrowly focused? Is the work large or small?

The audience is who you want the work to reach. Is the work for children or adults? Have you identified a target audience such as males 16-24 or is the work designed for a general audience?

You have probably seen Living Books line on CD ROM. A popular series in this line are the wonderful books by Mercer Mayer such as Just Grandma and Me, Just Me and My Dad, and Just For You. While children are the audience for the books, the publisher did not forget that Adults would be the ones purchasing the CD ROMs. For this reason, the purpose of the books is to provide educational entertainment to children. Given this purpose, the CD ROM editions of the print books are much larger in scope and were programmed with features to entertain and educate children. A key part of which was to allow children to interact with the publication or simply let the story be read to them.

The publisher did not forget the potential for an international audience for the CD ROM. Most Living Books allow you to select a language for the book to be read in such as English, Japanese or Spanish. This gives the CD ROMs international appeal and provides another educational outlet. Children in Japan could listen to the English version of the CD ROM to help them learn English. Children in the US could listen to the Spanish version to help them learn Spanish.

Researching

Researching involves gathering all the information you need to complete the work. This may mean gathering information about eighteenth-century Europe from as many sources as you can to ensure your work has elements authentic from the period. Or it may mean driving to the ocean to photograph or video tape the seagulls and the spray of the waves, so you can later capture the moment in your work.

Composing

Composing is the act of putting your thoughts into a more permanent form. This means putting work on paper or using computer equipment to put work into an appropriate digital form. You will most likely put words into a word processor, transcribe musical notes into a music program, and record brush strokes using a paint program.

The work as first put down on paper or recorded on a computer does not have to be the finished product. More than likely, it will simply be a start on a larger work. For the writer, a start on a project could be a few words, a list of thoughts, a paragraph, or pages of writing.

Evaluating

Evaluating involves looking at the work objectively to see if it meets your goals. Ask yourself if the work is right for the purpose and audience for which you are creating it. Often, the best way to be objective about a work you have created is to look at the work as if someone else had created it.

If you find that you cannot be objective about your own work or aren't as objective as you would like, perhaps you need to distance yourself from the work. Take a day off or put on one of your other hats and work on a different part of the project for a few days. This will help you return to the evaluation fresh and ready to think objectively.

Revising

When you revise, you change the structure of the work by adding, deleting, or rearranging. Often you will revise after you have evaluated the work. Revisions can be cosmetic changes involving only a few minor areas of the work, but more often than not, revision means major reworking to keep the work focused on the purpose, scope, and audience for which it is intended.

Editing

Whereas revision looks at the structure of the work, editing looks at the style, mechanics, and format of the work. For writing, this means making sure you have used proper spelling, grammar, and punctuation. You would check word choice and format. Great tools to help you through editing are spelling and grammar checkers. These tools might catch 75 percent of your mistakes, but the other 25 percent you will have to catch through careful reading.

During the editing stage, don't forget the non-written as aspects of your final product. You should also edit these aspects of the work as necessary. Ask yourself:

- Do the opening graphics match the tone and style of the graphics you selected in later sections of the work?

- Do the graphs and charts use consistent font faces, sizes and colors?
- Did you spell check the artwork?

Proofing

When you proof something, you are checking the final copy to ensure it is error-free. In traditional publishing, proofing has been a critical area of the composing process. Typos are costly mistakes to correct when material has already gone to press. In your writing, this may or may not be the case. You may be able to make changes very easily.

You may be saying to yourself, wait a minute, I have seen typos in publications before. While most publications have typos, they tend to make you look dumb. For this reason, you will want to correct as many typos as you can given the time constraints of the project.

Development Processes

The processes involved in developing the presentation aspects of the project can be broadly defined as *development processes*. Because the development processes are fairly complex, let's first explore what development means. Remember, you are handling your writing assignment as a project to improve your results and your success rate.

Any project, even a small one, can have very demanding requirements. To help you deal with those requirements and successfully deliver the work, you need to tackle the work as any professional would regardless of whether your work was assigned by a boss, professor, or editor.

No Composing/Programming Required

In the role of the graphic designer, musician, artist and programmer, you design and develop graphs, charts, diagrams, artwork, music, animation and whatever else is necessary to give the project a professional appearance.

It is important to note that if your project needs multimedia (recorded audio, animation, video, etc.), you may never have to resort to actually composing these multimedia aspects. Many wonderful tools are available to aid the development process and most word processors and presentation tools have all the basic bells and whistles you'll want to use.

Therefore, your programming/design role may be more closely related to that of a multimedia developer. You will be responsible for the look and interworkings of the work. You will also be responsible for selecting the appropriate software tools for your level of expertise and a software process model under which the project will be developed.

Fortunately, the software process model of choice will normally be a rapid prototype model or a modified rapid prototype model. This is because toolsets exist to aid in the rapid creation of multimedia projects and because these tools are of sufficient quality to warrant their use. The next section explains what these prototype models involve.

Using Development Models

A major strength of the rapid prototype model is that you can develop the project in linear fashion. You proceed from the working model to the finished product. You can test the prototype in real-world situations or under the scrutiny of the boss.

In doing so, you can ensure that what you are creating is what is actually needed. Applying this model to creative projects will also save you time.

The rapid prototype model also works well when you are familiar with traditional approaches to project development and are concerned about using new technologies or methods.

By developing a rapid prototype, you try out the tools to find out if they meet your needs and give yourself the chance to test the effectiveness of the multimedia you are adding to the work. This will help you manage the risk of introducing multimedia while allowing you to assess new techniques.

A modified rapid prototype model for creative projects could include six stages.

- Requirements phase
- Rapid prototype phase
- Specification phase
- Planning phase
- Design phase
- Implementation phase

As you read about each of these phases, it is important to remember that the duration of each phase should be relevant to the size and complexity of the publishing project. The initial project you create using this or any other model will require more time. For a small project or for subsequent projects, you probably could perform all the phases through the design phase in a single eight-hour day.

The implementation phase in multimedia projects tends to be the longest phase. Learning about the multimedia tools you have chosen will probably take up most of your time in your initial project, so the implementation phase may seem excessively long. It is important to remember that each subsequent time you use the tools should be easier than the last. The good news is that multimedia tools tend to be very user-friendly.

The wonderful thing about multimedia projects is that if you take the time to design a good product, you often can reuse some of the same specifications and designs in subsequent projects. This can give your reports, presentations and productions a uniform look, and as an added bonus the payoff in time savings will be substantial.

Finally, remember the rapid prototype model as a linear part of your project's development life cycle. Unlike the composing processes, each phase of the development process should be conducted in order.

Requirements Phase

In the requirements phase you try to figure out what your needs are. You do this by first examining the purpose, scope, and audience of the project. Afterward, you examine your reasonable expectations for the project. You translate these needs, goals, and purposes into requirements for the project.

While the section on techniques to get the project started provides a sample schedule that lists goals and milestones, the basic needs for any multimedia project include the tools you will need to complete the project.

- A drawing tool to create graphics.
- A sound tool to create or edit sound.
- A video tool to play or test video segments.

You will want to think beyond your basic tool needs. You should also consider time, budget and personnel constraints. If you have only 10 weeks to complete the project, you may need to bring in additional team members to get the project finished on time. In this case, getting a specific number of additional team members would be one of your requirements.

If you have a fixed budget, you will have to scrutinize every aspect of the budget to keep costs down. In this case, you will probably be extremely selective about the tools you purchase. You will also bring in outside help only as necessary. And if the budget constraints are so severe that they would materially affect the success of the project, you will want to ensure your superiors are aware of the situation and possibly make a case for getting a larger budget.

Rapid Prototype Phase

In the rapid prototype stage, you roll back your sleeves and dive right into the project. Using the requirements for the project, you create a working model of the finished product as quickly as possible. The prototype is far from a completed project. Its structure is rather skeletal in that not all the pieces are represented. You use this model to figure out your real needs and to find out whether you have selected the right tools to carry you through to the completion of the job.

The traditional school of thought on the rapid prototype model is that when you are done with this phase, you should discard the rapid prototype. If you do not discard the prototype you may find yourself wasting time trying to continually build and fix the prototype. The purpose of creating the rapid prototype is to help you figure out real needs and save you time. Clinging to the prototype generally defeats the purpose of creating the prototype in the first place.

If you show the prototype to your boss, professor or editor, make sure they understand what this phase is all about. All too often, the prototype is mistaken for a start on the final product. When in fact, it is not. You should manage expectations by ensuring your superiors understand this phase from day 1 and recommunicating information about the purpose of the prototype periodically throughout the project.

This said, in certain cases, you may want to keep parts of the prototype. You may want to reuse or refine for the finished product any creative work, such as charts, graphs, and pictures, you developed for the rapid prototype.

Specification Phase

After you develop and verify the prototype, you go on to specify the complete interworkings of the project. You could do this in a traditional manner through specification diagrams but these types of diagrams are not really necessary (unless you are writing actual programming code for the project). A good way to show the organization of the final product is to develop a storyboard that graphically shows what the pieces of the project are and how they are linked together. Storyboards are discussed in depth later.

In this phase, you will want to select a target computer that you will use for presenting the multimedia project (if this is required). Many types of computers are on the market. The IBM PC and PC compatibles have many generations of computer systems based on the different chip sets. Some PCs are based on Intel's Pentium chips. Some aren't. The same is true for Macintoshes—you might choose from a whole line of iMacs or MacBooks. UNIX systems come in many configurations from Sun Microsystems' popular Sparc workstations to Linux workstations.

The best system to use is the system you are most familiar with. You may not have a choice however. A professor may not allow you to bring in your laptop or corporate security rules may not allow outside computers.

Planning Phase

After you verify the specification documents, you should plan the project. Using all the materials you have developed so far for the project, you determine how long the project is going to take and the steps necessary to carry you through the project. For this reason, the planning phase can also be a reality check for project constraints or requirements.

For example, after you plan each step of the project you discover that it will take a minimum of 6 months to complete the project, yet the deadline for project completion given to you by management is 3 months away. Here, something would have to give and you would have to work hard to manage perceptions and expectations concerning the project. You may have to renegotiate the deadline, bring in additional team members or eliminate certain time-intensive parts of the project.

The more complex the project, the more involved your planning will be. The plans for a small project could be very basic, a list of steps with deadlines for completion of each step written down on a single piece of paper. The plans for a large project could be rendered in detail on a project management tool, such as Microsoft Project.

Most projects have windows for project steps, such as 8 days for planning or 3 weeks for preliminary design. There could be hundreds of project steps, with multiple steps being performed simultaneously or a handful of steps with each step being performed one after the other.

Some steps would be dependent on other steps, meaning they could not be started until certain other aspects of the project were completed. Other steps would not be dependent on any other steps and could be performed at any time during the project's development.

Design Phase

After verifying your planning, you go on to the design phase. The design phase is one of the most critical phases of a project. During this phase you take the specification documents to another level of detail. You develop the look of the project. You design the layout for the entire work and individual pages. By developing a master storyboard for the component parts of the entire work, you can make the design phase easier and less time-consuming.

The master storyboard concept is a highly effective way to design. Instead of creating hundreds of individual storyboards, you create templates for the major divisions of the project. These templates form the basis for individual storyboards. In this way, you have to make only minor adjustments to the individual storyboards and you get a uniform look throughout major sections of the work.

Implementation Phase

After you verify the designs you have created, you go on to the implementation phase. This tends to be the longest phase because you will actually create the work using the specification and designs you have created. You will also integrate the creative materials from the composing processes in this stage.

Pre-Finalization Processes

The processes involved in producing the finished product can be broadly defined as *pre-finalization processes*. In the role of the editor and producer, you fine tune the work to make it a more viable product. You must take a hard look at the project through the eyes of an editor, and then take the project through the final four activities.

- Revision
- Editing
- Proofing
- Testing

These activities are very similar to the associated activities performed in the composition process. The primary difference is in your role. You should no longer view yourself as the creator of the work or a collaborator of the work. You must review the project objectively and as if through another's eyes.

Revision

During the revision phase, you are looking for major flaws in the completed work. The focus of revision is on structure. You will reanalyze the individual parts of the project to ensure the work is focused and consistent throughout. To do this, you might also have to reevaluate the purpose, scope, and audience for the project.

Ask yourself:

- Did the project turn out as intended?
- Is the project larger or more viable than the original concept?
- Is the project still targeted toward the same audience?

When you revise the project you should scrutinize all its parts from start to finish. The soundness of structure is extremely important.

The depth of the revision often depends on your familiarity with the subject and type of project. If this is your first project or you are creating a new type of work you will want to use a very thorough revision process. A good technique to follow when doing a very thorough revision is the *rule of three*.

Under the rule of three you follow all aspects of the completed work from start to finish three times. Each time you revise, you are looking for different structure problems.

The first time through the process you check for clarity and content. Ask yourself:

- Is everything in the work clear?
- Are the text aspects of graphics easy to read and placed on the page in a clear manner?
- Does the content of each individual part fit in with the work as a whole?

The first revision is the closest inspection of the work during the revision process.

The second time, you look at the organization and layout of the work. Ask yourself:

- Is the work organized in the best way possible?
- Is the layout of the work the best possible?
- Is there too much information?
- Do pages look cluttered?
- Are the navigation mechanisms (table of contents, index, etc.) easy to use?

The third time, analyze the work to see if the overall message meets the proposed purpose and audience. Look at the big picture and ask yourself:

- Is the work right for the purpose for which it is intended?
- Is the reading level and style of the work appropriate for the audience for which it is intended?

Editing

Editing should logically follow revision. There is no point in looking for mechanics and format problems in parts of the work that might not be in the revised work. Keeping this rule in mind when you start the pre-finalization process will ultimately save you time.

Back in the editing mode, you look at the mechanics and format of the work. This is the point when you should refer to a style manual to ensure punctuation, capitalization, and compounding of words are correct. Other good tools at this point include grammar reference aids, bad speller dictionaries, and other types of dictionaries or reference materials to confirm facts.

In a large work such as a thesis paper or a dissertation, the tendency is to look at chapter text and not the text of titles and headings. Look at all text no matter where it appears in the work. If graphics or video contain text, you should scrutinize this text as well. There should be smooth transitions between sections and topics. The capitalization in headings should be consistent throughout the work.

For the textual portions of the work you should look at:

- Capitalization
- Grammar
- Punctuation
- Sentence structure
- Spelling
- Word choice and usage

Proofing

At this stage, you proof the entire project down to the most minor detail. The most common type of error you will be looking for are typos. In non-professional work, typos may not be costly in terms of money, but they can still ruin an otherwise great product.

The proofing stage differs from the revision stage and the editing stage in its scope.

- In revision, you are looking for major problems in structure.
- In editing, you are looking for problems in mechanics and format.
- In proofing, you are looking through a magnifying glass for minor problems.

Although these three processes can be performed in any order, they work best when done in order. In this way, you are first looking at the big picture, and then you gradually pan in. Otherwise, you will spend too much time worrying needlessly about minor details before you look at the major problems.

When you proof something you are checking the final copy to ensure it is as error-free as possible. You should recognize that given your time and budget constraints, you may have to compromise accuracy for timeliness. You should also recognize there is a definite point of diminishing returns and that finding 100% of the errors is costly and often not practical. For this reason, most finished works contain typos and other types of minor errors. Therefore, the key to proofing is to reduce these errors and not necessarily eliminate them.

Testing

Once the project is in its final form, you may want to produce a limited number of samples. The purpose of creating samples based on the finished project is to view the work in final form.

For printed works, such as a report, thesis or essay, this means printing out the work just as you will submit it. Turn off draft mode on your printer, use color (if used) and full sheets of paper. Print out the title page and all other pages.

For other works, such as a presentation, e-book or CD ROM, this means going through a complete delivery test.

- Do a practice presentation in the board room.
- View the e-book on different computers with different size monitors and display modes.
- Burn the project to CD ROM in full form and test it on several computers.

If this is your first project of this type, you may want to conduct extensive testing. You might also want to conduct extensive testing if you are publishing for the first time in a new medium.

Combining It All

Ideally, during the publication process you would follow the composing processes for the project first. When you finished, you would start the development phases. Finally, you would start the pre-finalization processes. Although this is the ideal situation, life is never ideal. Often, you will want to combine elements from each of the three categories and work on them simultaneously. This is fine.

You can conduct the composition process while you are developing the multimedia aspects of the project. This will work especially well when you are adapting existing material. It will also work well when you are collaborating with writers, musicians, or artists to create a project.

The pre-finalization processes are more difficult to integrate into the ongoing creation and development of the project. Yet, you could create or develop pieces of the project, and then examine those pieces from the viewpoint of the objective pre-finalization processes.

Exercise caution when trying to perform all three processes at once. The tendency is to gloss over the actual pre-finalization process and not scrutinize the project as closely or objectively as you otherwise would have.

Chapter 4: Techniques to Get Started

To organize a project you must start the project. Getting the project started is often the hardest thing to do. If you get the project started, the odds are you will probably finish the project. The key to starting the project and finishing the project is to develop good habits for working on the project immediately.

Setting a Schedule

Creative people often find themselves at a loss for one of two reasons. They either prefer to avoid work until a deadline is hanging over their head or they think of reasons why they cannot work.

Human tendency is to put off work until it absolutely has to be done or to think of excuses why the project cannot be started. Procrastination is a mind-set that you can overcome through positive thinking and good habits. If you find that you work on the project only when absolutely necessary to meet a deadline or if you keep promising to start the project but do not, try the following:

Give yourself a schedule. The schedule should contain milestones, goals, and an allocation of time. Use the schedule as a flexible and realistic guideline to help you through to project completion. The purpose of the schedule is to help you start thinking about the project and to formalize the steps it will take you to complete the project. You should also use the schedule to help you set regular times to work on the project.

Milestones

Milestones are generally smaller in scope than goals. A single week could contain many milestones; for example:

Week 1

- Select and purchase reference materials
- Select and purchase necessary software
- Brainstorm
- Develop weekly schedule overview

Week 2

- Browse the reference materials to gather ideas
- Freewrite
- Develop weekly schedule
- Develop project outline

Week 3

- Track down necessary resources
- Build project team chart
- Create contact list
- Start gathering data

Week 4

- Create a synopsis or executive summary
- Determine charts, graphs, and graphics needed
- Develop structure of draft 1

Goals

Goals are larger in scope than milestones. Goals for a typical project could be to complete activities or phases in the composition, development, or pre-finalization processes. Goals are generally of long duration. You would probably only have one goal per week during the project, such as the following:

Weekly Goals

- Week 1: Preliminary work on project
- Week 2: Planning
- Week 3: Research
- Week 4: Start project composition

Connecting Milestones and Goals

More realistically, the duration of milestones and goals will depend on the time you allocate to the project. The milestones and goals from the previous examples could be rewritten to include the time you will dedicate to the project each week and the duration of a task.

While it would be ideal to be able to work full-time on a single project, even full-time writers don't have that luxury very often. Usually they are juggling several projects and can only dedicate a few hours a week to any specific project. If you are working part-time on the project, one of your first goals may be broken down as follows:

Goal: Preliminary work on project.

Duration: 2 weeks.

Week 1: 10 hours

- Select and purchase reference materials. Duration: 2 hours.
- Select and purchase software. Duration: 2 hours.
- Brainstorm. Duration: 2 hours.
- Create preliminary outline and goals: 2 hours.
- Develop weekly schedule overview. Duration: 1 hour.
- Slack time: 1 hour.

Week 2: 20 hours

- Browse the reference materials to gather ideas. Duration: 3 hours.
- Expand outline and goals: 2 hours.
- Freewrite. Duration: 1 hour.
- Develop weekly schedule. Duration: 8 hours.
- Start project, complete at least one page. Duration: 3 hours.
- Slack time: 3 hours.

Slack time is good! There is no harm in building extra time into the schedule to ensure you meet goals. The above schedule contains 1 hour of slack time in the first week and 3 hours of slack time in the second week.

By building slack time into the schedule, you help ensure the project can stay on track even if there are unexpected delays. Experienced project managers try to build in slack time whenever possible and practical.

When you meet a goal, why not celebrate? Take a few hours off, go see that movie you have wanted to see.

Chapter 5: Techniques to Organize for the Audience

The way in which you organize a project largely depends on who will be seeing/reading the finished work. The success of your project relies on determining the audience and adapting the message to the audience. You will certainly organize the project one way for adults and a different way for children. However, the audience for a work is usually not in such simple terms.

Defining the Audience

The problem of determining the audience is further complicated because most creative endeavors have more than one audience. Yet, correctly determining the target audience can have huge payoffs.

The target audience could be specific, males 16-24, or general, young adults. More often, a work will have primary audiences and secondary audiences. The primary audience is the group of people for whom the work is created. The focus and thrust of the work should be directed toward the primary audience.

The secondary audience is the group of people who will see/read the finished work incidental to its purpose. The secondary audience could include reviewers (people whose job it is to review the work), consumer interest groups (people whose job it is to promote the interests of consumers), or anyone else who might see/read the work to determine its quality or to review its content. The secondary audience could also include parents if the work is directed toward children.

Parents may be the ones ensuring the moral content of the work before purchasing it for their children.

Often, the primary audience for a work seems straightforward but is not. Comic books are a good example of this. The reading level of the average comic book is at a sixth-grade level. The look of comic books with their graphically depicted pows, bangs, and booms seem to be directed entirely toward children. You may be surprised to learn that for many comic books, the largest percentage of readers is adults.

Look at the price tag on comic books today and the phenomenal popularity of comic books with adult themes. What would have happened to comic books if the companies producing them had not realized that a large portion of their readers are adults?

You can figure out the audience for your publication by the following means:

- Seeing with the reader's eyes
- Gathering statistics
- Evaluating trends

> **Reality Check:** *Selling a product doesn't always involve a monetary transaction. Never forget that you have to work hard to "sell" any type of product, even one that is given away for free or presented to peers. You sell an audience with your approach and finished product.*

Seeing With the Reader's Eyes

One of the best tools to analyze the audience for a product is to try to see with the readers eyes. Realize the audience probably will not have the same wants, needs, and desires as you. A work in one form may or may not have the same audience in another form.

Try to put yourself in the position of consumers who will see/read the work. Use what you know about people and what you know about the subject of your work to predict likely responses to these questions, such as the following:

- What will the reader's initial reaction be?
- What will the reader's expectations be?
- What does the reader consider interesting?
- What features will the reader be looking for?
- What are the "selling" points for this type of work?
- How will the reader use your work?
- What reading level should you target?
- What level of violence or profanity is acceptable to this audience? (if any)
- What level of complexity in the navigation mechanisms and presentation is acceptable?

Each of these questions should be answered with the project's audience in mind. For example, the last question pertains to the complexity of the work. Publications for adults tend to be more complex and serious. Publications for children tend to be less complex and include more entertainment features.

Gathering Statistics

One of the best ways to determine your audience is to use statistics. Sometimes you can simply ask consumers, peers, etc. what they are looking for or looking to gain by seeing/reading the work. You could do this through a carefully designed survey. Other times, you might want to use existing statistics, such as demographic information, to determine the audience.

Surveys

Surveys are often an inexpensive way to learn people's opinion. Surveys could be provided with samples passed out at the campus library or given to your associates. Surveys are useful because they can be filled out by many people at the same time. A properly designed survey will be easy to answer and not time-consuming. This way, more people will fill out the survey.

Demographics

Demographic information can also provide useful statistics. Demographic information includes age, sex, race, education level, income, and more. This data was probably gathered through surveys and made publicly available.

Not all the demographic information available will be relevant to your needs, but some of the data will be extremely important. For instance, if the demographic information reveals most of the consumers buying/reading your type of product are females age 40-45 or males over the age of 55, you would certainly produce a different work than if the information reveals the ages are 20-25 for females or 16-22 for males.

You can also look several places on the World Wide Web to find demographic data. This data covers a wide range of topics from many sources, ranging from the Census Bureau to public interest groups.

Evaluating Trends

Evaluating trends could also help you determine an audience for your product. To evaluate trends, you will have to know something about the market for your product. You could begin by looking at similar works and asking yourself the following:

- What message do the works carry?
- Toward what target audience are these works directed?
- Are the works being targeted toward secondary audiences as well?

In a new marketplace, trends often shift as individuals and companies try to figure out the audience for their products. You may want to look at what others are doing when you begin work on the project and again during the project. This way you can judge if the trend is more stable than fluid or more fluid than stable.

Chapter 6: Organizing Through Storyboarding

A *storyboard* can help you reduce complexity by structuring ideas in a less complicated manner. When you storyboard, you represent each page of the presentation in miniature form on a planning sheet. This enables you to visualize the work from start to finish.

Being able to see the component parts of the entire project makes the project more manageable and less mysterious. You do not have to wonder what is beyond the next page because when you use the storyboards you will know what is beyond the next page.

Working with Storyboards

You can represent a single project storyboard as a rectangle where the shape of an individual storyboard makes it look like a little piece of paper. Individual storyboards can represent a single page of the work or a group of similar pages, like a chapter.

Understanding Storyboards

Without information in the storyboards, the mockup of the project you create would have little meaning. You can add information to storyboards such as chapter headings or titles where the basic idea is to create a template or outline for pages or sections of the publication.

You can extend the idea of storyboards by using lines and

arrows to show how the finished product is linked or navigated. An arrow can show the flow from one page/section to the next. Arrows depict how the component parts of the publication link together. By examining the links you can see the logical structure of the work.

Developing storyboards is a critical part of the design process. Storyboards help ensure the project is well-designed and that all the pieces of the project fit together. After you have developed the storyboard for the work, you can immediately find flaws in the design. Finding flaws early in the development of the project will save you time and resources.

Having to rebuild the organization in a complex project midway through could mean disaster. Often, you start a snowball effect. You move one section, and then discover you have to change another section. You change that section, and then find other things you have to change.

Before you know it, you are reworking the organization of the entire project. At this point, the process may be so involved you will elect to start over rather than try to rework the project.

Designing Your Storyboard

The storyboard design process has three phases. These phases involve:

- Developing the storyboard structure
- Developing the storyboard content
- Evaluating the logic of the storyboard

Each phase is progressively more detailed.

When you are developing the structure of the project you are looking at the project overview level. While keeping in mind that a single storyboard could represent any number of similar pages, you identify the number of storyboards for the project and the logical flow between them.

When you are developing the content, you look very closely at the individual parts of the project. You develop the outline for individual storyboards or storyboard templates.

When you examine the logic of the project you scrutinize every detail of the project. You closely examine each storyboard and all links to ensure the project design and flow is correct.

Completing the Design

Whether you perform each of the three phases will depend on the size and complexity of the project and your familiarity with the type of project you are working on. However, each phase that you do perform should be performed in sequence.

Even a small project of 5-10 storyboards can benefit from the structural development phase. This way, you will have an easy way to see

- The structure of the project
- The links of the project—its navigation and flow
- The project as a whole

Although these phases should be performed in order, the important thing to remember is that the duration of each phase should be relevant to the size and complexity of the project.

The initial project you create using this or any other model will require more time than subsequent projects. For a small project or for subsequent projects, you probably could create the entire storyboard process in two hours or less.

If you take the time to design a good storyboard, you may be able to reuse some of the same design concepts in subsequent projects. This way your projects will have a uniform structure.

An added bonus to using reliable design techniques is substantial time-savings and a reduction in the amount of resources you will need to complete the project.

Developing Structure Using Storyboards

Developing the structure of the project is the first phase in storyboarding. You can organize storyboards in many ways. The structure that is best for your publication depends on the complexity of the project. As complexity increases, you manage it by adopting a more advanced structuring method. Specific design models include

- Linear – traditional writing, such as essays, novels and articles
- Linear with alternative paths – textbooks and technical guides
- Hierarchical – complex presentations, digital media

Linear Structure

For a small project or project with limited complexity, a simple structure is often best. Simple structures include linear and linear with alternative paths.

The simplest way to structure a publication is in a *linear* fashion. Using a pure linear structure, you can create a publication with a traditional structure. Readers move in sequence through the pages of the publication.

Most articles, essays and novels have a similar linear organization. They begin with an introduction, continue with the main text, and end with a summary.

An *alternative path linear* structure gives readers more options or paths through the finished work. By providing alternative paths, you make the structure of the publication more flexible. Instead of being able to move in sequence through the publication, readers can follow a branch from the main path. Think textbook where the book has a table of contents, index and cross references for easy access.

Here, readers could start with Chapter 1 and read in sequence. They could also refer to the table of contents, the index, or cross references to find topics of interest. This allows readers to skip around the work as necessary to answer their questions.

Hierarchical Structure

The *hierarchical* structure is the most logical structure for complex presentations and digital media. In this structure, you organize the work into a directory tree. Readers can navigate through the work moving from one level of the publication to the next, more detailed, level of the publication. They can also go up the tree from the detailed level to a higher level and possibly jump to the top level.

The directory tree closely resembles the way you store files on your hard drive in a main directory with subdirectories leading to files. You could also think of the hierarchy as a representation of an actual tree. If you invert the tree, the trunk of the tree would be the top level of the publication.

The trunk could be the overview of the publication. The large boughs leading from the trunk would be the next level of the document structure. The boughs could be the chapter overview pages. Branches leading from the boughs would be the next level. They could be pages within chapters.

A hierarchical structure is extremely logical. Using the branches of the inverted tree, readers can navigate through the document. The seamless and easy movement from one level of the publication to the next, more detailed, level is what makes the hierarchical structure so useful. Readers know precisely where they are in the publication. They know that if they descend through the structure, they will get more detailed information, and if they go back up the structure they will find less detailed information.

Hierarchical organization is commonly used with lists or menus. An upper-level storyboard containing a chapter index or a list of major topics would form the menu. The reader could select one of the menu items to read a chapter or a particular topic. If the publication is a collection of topics, the first menu could take the reader to an additional menu with subtopics.

To give readers an easy way to navigate the hierarchical structure, you can use three mechanisms.

- A feature to go down the structure
- A feature to go up the structure
- A feature to jump to a specific overview level of the publication

To keep the user interface consistent, you should provide these three basic navigation mechanisms throughout the publication. There are some exceptions to this rule. On the first storyboard, you would only provide a way for readers to go down the hierarchy. On a bottom-level storyboard you would only provide a way for readers to go up the hierarchy or to jump to a specific overview level.

Be careful not to provide too many levels in the document. This is particularly a problem when the publication contains topic and subtopic menus. If readers have to progress through six levels of menus before they get to any real information, they are going to get frustrated. To eliminate this problem, try to limit both the number of levels and the number of menu choices wherever possible. You may also want to start the readers on an index page.

Developing Content Using Storyboards

Now that you have developed the structure of the storyboards you will want to look closer at the individual parts of the project. Developing the content of the storyboards will help you do this. The depth of the content development really depends on the size and complexity of the project.

A traditional way to develop a small project is to develop all content aspects of the storyboard, from the placement of graphics to the placement of text. Similarly, the traditional development method for a large storyboard is to outline each individual storyboard and then progressively work toward more detail as necessary. A better method is to use storyboard templates or master storyboards whenever possible and develop individual storyboards only as necessary.

Developing Master Storyboards

Master storyboards are a highly effective way to design. They make the design process considerably less complex and will save you countless hours of work. Instead of creating hundreds of individual storyboards, you create templates for the major divisions of the project. These templates form the basis for the individual storyboards. In this way, you have to make only minor adjustments to the individual storyboards, and you ensure the look of the work is consistent throughout.

The main idea behind master storyboards is that you identify repetitious or non-unique features of the publication and let a single master storyboard represent pages in the work with like features. You do this by looking at the work in progressive levels of detail. Most works will have the following:

- Overview pages
- A table of contents
- Topic or chapter overview pages
- Pages within chapters or topics
- An index

Start by thinking about the work as a whole. Are there component parts of the work that will or should be uniform throughout?

The answer is usually yes because the top of the page will contain a header consistent throughout the work and the bottom of the page will contain a footer consistent throughout the work.

Next, examine the sections of the work. Multiple sections of the work will usually have common components, such as introduction, body and summary.

The last step is to examine individual sections of the work for common material. Pages of an index will contain different features or organization from pages of a chapter. But all pages within a chapter or within an index should have similar elements.

After you have examined all aspects of the work, you develop the master storyboards. You may have multiple levels of master storyboards.

- An overall master storyboard
- A master storyboard that can be used in multiple sections
- A master storyboard for individual sections

You may have only one or many master storyboards. The number of master storyboards you have really depends on the size and complexity of your project.

Developing Individual Storyboards

In the design stage, you will rarely develop individual storyboards. This is especially true if you take the time to develop master storyboards.

Whether you develop individual storyboards depends on the needs of the project. For a small project you may want to develop all the storyboards so you get a precise overview of the work. For a large project you may make only simple additions to the individual storyboards, like adding the chapter title or page numbers for associated text.

Sometimes it is essential to develop the content for unique storyboards within the work to see how they will fit in with the work as a whole. You develop these storyboards because through them, you can get a better understanding of the work.

The following are examples of unique storyboards:

- Title page
- Table of contents page
- Chapter index page
- Acknowledgements page

Evaluating Storyboard Organization

In the last phase of storyboarding, you evaluate the logic of the storyboard you created. This process is similar to the editing, revision, and proofing activities of the pre-finalization process.

You examine the links between storyboards. You ensure the work has a logically flowing structure and that all storyboards are properly linked together. Then you examine the outlines the storyboards contain. Here, you are primarily making sure the key elements are placed on the storyboard in the most logical manner.

The storyboarding process is meant to save time, resources, and frustration. Do not spend too much time worrying needlessly about minor details. Look only for major problems in logic.

Part I: Quick Review

The best creative works are the result of effective strategies for thinking, planning, and composing. Helping you develop the best writing using effective strategies is what this section was all about.

- You set yourself on the path to success by managing expectations, perceptions, strategies, goals, rules, and behavior.

- You improve your initial ideas through brainstorming, freethinking, and storyboarding.

- You convince yourself to stop procrastinating by setting a flexible and realistic schedule containing milestones, goals, and an allocation of time to help you through to project completion.

- You figure out who the audience for the work is by seeing through the reader's eyes, gathering statistics, and evaluating trends.

- You tackle the project and progress through the composition, development, and pre-finalization processes.

- You reduce complexity in project design by visualizing the work from start to finish using storyboards. Being able to see the component parts of the entire project makes the project more manageable and less mysterious.

Before you continue, try one of the following exercises:

Exercise 1

Your boss, professor or editor has asked you to write a feature article about holidays and traditions. The article should trace the history around your favorite holidays or traditions, and should help the reader envision the magic that started it all.

The article must be 8,000 words and include artwork depicting how the holiday or tradition has developed over the years.

You are also responsible for the layout of the article and your work will be judged not only on the writing, but also the design.

The project is due 4 weeks from today. Use the techniques discussed in Part I of this book to create a project plan. The project plan should include multiple brainstorming or freewriting sessions out of which will come three deliverables:

- Schedule with goals and milestones.
- A storyboard of the feature article.
- A detailed review of the potential audience for this type of article.

Exercise 2

Your boss, professor or editor has given you a 10,000 word research assignment. To complete the assignment, you must write a research report on Heroes of the Renaissance, Renaissance Art, or Renaissance Literature, and use the report to develop a presentation. The presentation must be 1 hour long and include handouts.

The entire project is due 6 weeks from today. Use the

techniques discussed in Part I of this book to create a project plan. The project plan should include multiple brainstorming/freewriting sessions out of which will come three deliverables:

- A project schedule with goals and milestones.
- A storyboard of the report.
- A storyboard of the presentation.

Exercise 3

Your boss, professor or editor has given you a creative writing assignment. You are to write a fictional account of a journey onboard an 18th century sailing ship.

The story must be 8,000 words and must include drawings authentic to the day as well as diary/journal entries for the fictional hero/heroine of the story.

The entire project is due 3 weeks from today. Use the techniques discussed in Part I of this book to create a project plan. The project plan should include multiple brainstorming/freewriting sessions out of which will come three deliverables:

- A project schedule with goals and milestones.
- A storyboard of the story's organization or flow.
- A detailed review of the potential audience.

Part II: Page Design

Computer technology gives writers the freedom to provide information to readers in powerfully innovative ways. With this freedom comes opportunity, decisions and options. You have to consider how to organize the work, how to layout the work and how to design the pages of the work. You have already seen the many choices for organization. With layout and page design you'll encounter many more choices.

Pages with high visual impact will leave a lasting impression on readers. High visual impact does not necessarily correlate to high resolution graphics. Some of the most visually stunning pages contain no graphics at all. They achieve their impact from simplicity of design. They use screen space, color, fonts and headings to their advantage.

The best writing looks effortless. Words seem to flow straight from the writer's pen. The same is true about the best designed pages. Well-designed pages look effortless. They are organized in a way that is coherent and flowing.

The writer's secret to making words seem to flow effortlessly is simple. She knows that good work is the result of hard work—careful editing, revision and proofreading. Creating a single polished page may take hours. Well-designed pages are also the result of hard work. Designs that seem simple and natural to the reader are often the result of intense efforts to make them seem this way.

Chapter 7: Designing with Space

Sometimes it is not what you have on the page that helps convey your message, rather what you do not have on the page. Empty space on the page makes the material easier to read by drawing the reader's attention to the area of the page that has material on it.

It is the separation of material that creates emphasis and draws the reader's attention.

Using Space Effectively

Using space effectively is not a new idea. Graphic designers often balance the amount of empty space on a page to emphasize material. They do this by using wide margins whenever possible.

Open your favorite text book and you will probably find that the top margin is smaller than the bottom margin. Next compare the margins on two opposing pages. You may find that on the left-hand page the left margin is wide and the right margin near the binding is narrow. On the right-hand page the left margin near the binding is narrow and the right margin is wide.

Print publications are usually designed this way to make them more visually appealing.

Sizing Your Paragraphs

Another common spacing technique is to vary the length of paragraphs. If you use the same paragraph length repeatedly even the liveliest material can seem monotonous. You should use short paragraphs more often and restrict the use of long paragraphs.

A short paragraph has less than six lines. A long paragraph is more than 10 lines.

If you are designing for the Web, it is difficult to count lines. This is because the way you see the paragraph may not be the way the reader sees the paragraph. Yet by estimating that an average line may have 70 characters, you can also estimate the number of lines in a particular paragraph.

In the textual portion of your work you can use these traditional design techniques, yet you do not want to stop your good design techniques here. The material you provide or do not provide on the page is extremely important.

Adding Graphics

By adding a few graphics to the page you often can dramatically increase the page's impact. The images or features, such as charts and graphs, you add to the page do not have to be sophisticated or high-resolution.

Simple is almost always best. The placement of images and features on the page should be such that they focus the reader's attention to the primary textual portion of the page.

A page that is entirely graphical can also benefit from spacing techniques. If text is secondary to an image on the page, the center piece of the page should be the image. Then, you would design the page to enhance the value of the image.

The key is to use space in a way that enhances the design and draws attention to what you want to emphasize.

> ***Reality Check:*** *Test the spacing techniques you have chosen periodically during the writing to make sure they are effective. One of the quickest ways to do this is to use the Print Preview feature of the application you are using to compose the project. Printing all or parts of the project periodically doesn't hurt either—even if the ultimate destination for the work is digital media.*

Chapter 8: Understanding Color

The use of color in writing has always caused problems. In the early days of desktop publishing, people were discovering color printers.

Documents were printed in red, yellow, blue, purple and combinations of any other colors you can think of. This was not done because it was a sound design technique, rather because the desktop publisher could.

What Does Color Represent?

Color carries with it certain connotations. In the United States, red suggests danger, yellow suggests caution and green suggests all is clear.

Red could also represent hot. Blue could represent cold. To different groups of people these colors carry entirely different connotations. On Wall Street, red means losing money. To doctors, blue means death.

Colors that mean certain things in one country carry completely different connotations in other countries. Red can suggest aristocracy or masculinity in France, blasphemy in some African countries and in Korea, red can suggest death because red ink is used to record deaths.

In the US black is the color of mourning, yet in Korea, white is the traditional color of mourning. Yellow suggests grace in Japan, prosperity in Egypt and caution or cowardice in the US.

Therefore the key to using color and ensuring appropriate

appeal for your work is to make sure you are not using color to carry a hidden meaning to the reader.

Using Color in Presentations

For presentations, common computer graphic modes will allow you to use thousands of colors on the same screen. Some graphic modes will let you use millions of colors. With this many choices, there are bound to be problems.

This is especially true when you use color combinations with text and backgrounds. For example, lightly colored text against a white background is almost always a poor combination.

For presentations or visuals, the best rules to follow when using colorful text or backgrounds are

- Use basic colors for text, like black, gray, red, yellow, green, blue, and white.

- Use basic colors for background but contrast them with the text colors. For example, if you use a dark blue background, try using white, bright yellow, or black text.

- Do not use too many different color combinations with text and background colors on the same page. A text window with a blue background and yellow text and a text window with a green background and white text on the same page may clash.

- More than four different colors for text and backgrounds can also cause problems.

- Using color with graphic images can also cause problems. A photograph may look fantastic in your word processor, but not in print or as shown through a projector.

  Reality Check: Color on screen and color in print can be very different. Professional designers use color charts to make sure colors appear in print exactly as they expect. In most cases, if you are composing work for print, you'll be asked to ensure that you use CMYK colors rather than RGB. CMYK is a 4-color combination created with Cyan, Magenta, Yellow and Black, and designed primarily for printing presses. RGB is a 3-color combination created with Red, Green and Blue and is designed primarily for computer screens.

  Problems with color don't only occur in print. Whenever you develop presentations, you should be very aware of possible color issues as well. Projectors may not display colors as they appear on your computer screen. The vividness and clarity of color depends on the projector (and the projection backdrop).

Chapter 9: Powerful Headings

Headings are words or phrases that divide chapters or topics of the work into sections or subtopics. Headings are used to break up the page. A page broken into topics looks more manageable and interesting.

Headings help readers envision the organization of the publication at a glance by identifying main points. They also help readers quickly find topics of interest.

Headings: Best Uses

Normally, you will find that nonfiction works contain many headings and fiction works relatively few. Fiction works generally break down the publication by chapter or story. Nonfiction works generally break down the subject into topics and subtopics.

Breaking down the subject into manageable pieces is critically important, especially for difficult material. Studies have shown that our short-term memories can handle only seven plus or minus two pieces of information.

The rule of seven plus or minus two pieces of information is known as *Miller's law*. A piece of information does not necessarily correlate to a single word. Usually it represents concepts or ideas.

A paragraph could represent a single idea. This is why the optimum grouping of paragraphs under headings is three to seven paragraphs.

Good Headings vs. Bad Headings

One word headings are usually poor choices. Good headings explain what the topic is and convey information to the reader. Your headings could be a few words, a complete sentence or a question.

You can use different heading sizes to create levels of headings. Thus the largest heading size would be your first level heading and the smallest heading size would be your lowest level heading.

While you could create as many heading levels as you want, in general, you should only use three or four levels of headings.

> ***Reality Check:*** *Creating good headings is somewhat of an art. Often, the type of heading you use in one style of writing isn't the same as the type of heading you'll use in a different style of writing. If you are doing professional work, always study current examples. Sometimes, the preference will be on using action verbs in headings. Other times, the preference may be to use noun phrases. For example, you would choose the heading: Using Headings Effectively rather than Effective Headings. Subtle difference yes, but a difference that will be important to someone.*

Chapter 10: Exploring Fonts

The font you use defines the way text looks. When publications were typeset for a printing press, the number of fonts publishers used were limited. Each new font included in the publication cost the publisher money. Some companies specializing in creating fonts, charged thousands of dollars for a single font and because of this, even in the early days of computing, fonts were still expensive.

Thankfully, this is not true today. The power of type was unleashed in the early days of the desktop publishing revolution. Now, you can buy fonts for pennies, and there are thousands to choose from.

Working with Fonts

Fonts have many different characteristics. Some fonts, called screen or plotter fonts, look one way on the screen and print out another. Some fonts, called outline or scaleable fonts, look the same on-screen and on paper.

> **Reality Check** When your work will be viewed on a computer screen or projector, you probably do not care how text would look if it were printed out. However, keep in mind that handouts often accompany presentations and the easiest handout to make is a simple printout of the presentation.

Beyond this there are other characteristics common to all font types. You can use normal type, bold type, italic type and bold italic type. These different font types add emphasis and carry meanings. Italics can convey a sense of nostalgia. Bold type seems to be shouting at you.

Normal, bold and italic type form a basic font family. A font family is a group of related fonts. For most purposes each font type in a font family is counted as a separate font. This means if you purchase a font pack that claims to have 500 fonts, you will not get 500 different type faces. What you will get is several hundred font families with each font family generally having 3 font types (normal, bold, italic) or 4 font types (normal, bold, italic, bold italic).

> **Reality Check** *You may be wondering why underline is not included as a common characteristic of all font types. Underline is not included because it is a feature that can be added to any type of font and is not a characteristic of fonts.*

Deciding Which Font to Use

There are decorative fonts, heading fonts, fancy fonts, symbol fonts, and standard fonts. The problem with this many fonts is what font should you use in your work? To answer this, let's look at some font basics:

- Monospace vs. Proportional Type
- Font Size

- Font Styles

Monospace vs. Proportional type

The kind of type that most typewriters use is monospace type. In monospace type, each letter, number or symbol takes up the same space. A monospaced l takes as much space as a monospaced w. This is very easy to read and great for tired eyes. Monospaced type is still in wide use.

Another kind of type is proportional type. With proportional type, each letter, number or symbol takes up only the space it needs. Today, most fonts are proportional. Using proportional type, you can create variety and thus get more visual impact.

Although both proportional and non-proportional fonts are available, in most cases, you'll want to use proportional fonts to add visual variety to the main text and use non-proportional fonts only when you want the text to stand out clearly.

For example, you would use proportional fonts in headings and the main text and non-proportional text in source code examples of a technical manual.

Font Sizes

Fonts come in many sizes. The larger the type size, the larger the type. Font size is specified in units called points. A point is a printing unit that equals approximately 1/72 inch. However, the true size of the point really depends on how the font was designed.

Words in 10-point type using one font may not be the same as words in 10-point type in another font. This ambiguity in font sizes is something computers and desktop publishing have brought to the art of printing.

The most common point size for material designed to be read is 12-point. This is a good size for the main textual portions of any printed work. Other common sizes range from 9 to 12 for the main text.

When determining the size of the type to use, use a size that is easy to read. Remember, the readers' eyes may get tired. Do not make the type size so small they have to squint to read. Do not make type size so large that they feel they have to sit across the room to read either.

Font Styles

Fonts come in thousands of styles given names by their designers. Each font style, called a font family, will have different type sizes and should include normal, bold, italic and bold italic fonts.

Many font styles in use today are hundreds of years old. Fonts like Baskerville have been around since 1766. Some types that are considered modern first appeared over 200 years ago. Others like Castellar, Contemporary Brush and BriemScript have only been around for a few decades.

The name of a font sometimes conveys a message about the style of the font, but not always. Fonts like Ransom, Futura, Century Gothic, and NuptialScript carry distinct messages about the style. Fonts like New Century School Book, Contemporary Brush, Courier New and Times New Roman all seem to be saying they are modern.

Thousands of other font styles simply have a name that may or may not convey a meaning to you.

The font you choose for the main text does not have to be the font you chose to use in headings. Some fonts were meant to be used in headings. Some fonts were designed to be decorative. Other fonts were designed to be used in normal text.

The key to selecting a good font style is to use a font that is easy to read under a variety of conditions and works well for the purpose for which you plan to use it.

> **Reality Check** *A key concept in using fonts in your writing is to limit the number of font styles you use on any one page. For the sake of consistency, you should also limit the number of fonts you use throughout a complete work. A good rule of thumb is to use no more than three different font styles on any page and if possible and practical, use the same fonts throughout a complete work.*

Chapter 11: Unleashing Page Layout

To unleash the page, you must examine the page critically. Look deep into its design and not its words.

- What does your project have going for it besides its words?
- Does it follow a logical style and layout?
- Do the pages themselves make a statement?

How Graphic Designers Use Grids

The grid system is a way of designing pages that will help you create a uniform and symmetrical look to the published page. Graphic designers have used the grid system to design pages for many years.

Using the grid system, you would break the page into imaginary grid columns. Text, graphics and other objects on the page are lined up within the grid columns to give a consistent, clear look to the work.

A simple page could be broken into three grid columns. Complex pages could be divided into 10 or more grid columns.

The number of imaginary grid columns depends on the type and number of objects you are placing on the page. For example, a newsletter could be divided into three grid columns:

- Header and title information could go across the whole top of the page, meaning this text would be in all three grids.

- Pictures could be aligned in the first or leftmost grid one under the other down the page.

- Text could be placed in grid columns two and three.

While the grid system is used primarily in print projects, it also makes sense to use the grid system in digital projects. Your project should not look like an angry mess on the reader's computer screen.

The pages of your work should be pleasing to look at. Using the grid system can help you add symmetry to your pages.

Text Components in Page Design

Text is the most basic page component. Almost every page you create will contain some text. This will be true even for pages that are highly graphical in nature. Most pages of your work will include text in heading or title lines at the top or bottom of the page.

Another concern when you are placing text on the page is the type of alignment you use. In some cases, you may want to justify margins, meaning text on the right side of the page will be evenly lined up.

Justifying the text may allow you to cram more material on the page—up to 25% more text. It gives a uniform and professional look to the publication as well.

While justified margins make the finished product look better, they mean more work. This remains true though most word processors will let you create justified text by simply selecting all text and turning text justification on.

Justified text will not work well with non-proportional text. If all your text is in a non-proportional font, you probably will have to convert the text to a proportional font before using justified margins.

Justified text can leave gaping holes in your text. For lines of the page containing roughly half the character width of the page, you may see large areas with no text where the short line was stretched to fill the page width. You must fix each of these lines by hand or try to rework the paragraph.

If you choose to rework the paragraph, you have three options:

- You could rewrite the paragraph, changing words or word order, to make the paragraph work better with justification.
- You could try to break large words up using hyphenation.
- Or you could try both the rewriting and hyphenation techniques.

Graphic Components in Page Design

Graphics are another basic page component. Almost every work you create will contain some graphics. This will be true even for works that are highly textual in nature.

Graphics on the page do not have to be dazzling images or photo-quality pictures. They can be basic charts and graphs that visually summarize what the reader has read or provide an overview of statistics.

The best graphics highlight or summarize.

When adding graphic features to your work, the best advice is to use moderation. A few extra graphics will make the work more lively and inviting. Too many graphics will make the final product look busy and uninviting.

Part II: Quick Review

Using the techniques described in this section, you can design works that have high visual impact. You can use:

Space

> Empty space on the screen makes the material easier to read. It is the separation of the material that creates emphasis and draws the reader's attention.

Color

> The use of color in publications has always caused problems. Use basic colors for text and backgrounds whenever possible.

Headings

> The optimum grouping of paragraphs under headings is three to seven paragraphs. Good headings explain what the topic is and convey information to the reader. Your headings could be a few words, a complete sentence or a question.

Fonts

> Use proportional fonts to add visual variety to the work and non-proportional fonts when you want the text to be very clear and easy to read. The most common point size for material designed to be read is 12-point. Remember, the font you choose for the main text, does not have to be the font you chose to use in headings.

Grids

The grid system is a way to design pages that will lend a uniform and symmetrical look to the published page. Both text and graphics can be aligned using the grid system. In some cases, you may want to justify text to improve the look of the work.

Before you continue, try one of the following exercises:

Exercise 1

Continuing the feature article assignment, design and write the first few pages of the article, making sure to add appropriately-sized placeholders for graphics. Afterward, create title and credits pages, an executive summary page and a synopsis page for the article.

Exercise 2

Continuing the research assignment, create skeleton documents for the report and presentation. These documents should use placeholder text and graphics to showcase the page layout techniques discussed in this section. The report and presentation must include a title page, table of contents, executive summary page, main text pages and reference pages.

Exercise 3

Continuing the creative writing assignment, develop the first few pages of the story. These pages must include placeholders for text, drawings and diary entries that showcase the page layout techniques discussed in this section. Afterward, create title and credits pages, an executive summary page and a synopsis page for the story.

Part III: Tapping into the Power of Multimedia

Multimedia is a $150 billion business and growing. At first glance, creating multimedia productions can seem daunting. Do not let this be the case. We will reduce its complexity by tackling the concept one step at a time. This section explores the multimedia options available today, teaching the essential background necessary for success. In this section you learn:

- What multimedia is
- What the multimedia industry standards are
- Considerations to make before adding multimedia
- Critical questions to ask to figure out multimedia needs

Chapter 12: Multimedia Bonanza

Books, journals, and magazines have pictures. Pictures are an important aspect of multimedia, but they are not the only aspect of multimedia. Multimedia productions come alive before your eyes because they include graphics, music, sound effects and video when necessary.

Recent innovations in multimedia are making it easier than ever to incorporate sounds and video into your work. Be aware, the same innovations making it easier to use multimedia in your work are also driving changes in the marketplace.

Millions of people around the globe have seen what modern computers are capable of. We are buying faster, more powerful computers. We are installing sound cards, video cards and CD-ROM drives. All in an effort to get the best and most powerful computer on the block. And we not only want multimedia in the products we purchase, we demand it.

If used properly, multimedia can be the living aspect of your work. It is the spark that makes the work come alive. Instead of sitting through another boring presentation, you become a part of the experience.

If you talk about sound or video tools to initiates, they will bombard you with so many terms you will think they're talking a whole different language, for surely it is not English.

Thankfully, there are concepts common to both the sound and video aspects of multimedia.

By learning a few of these common concepts, you will have a better understanding of multimedia and multimedia tools. We will first take a look at the industry standards in multimedia, including JPEG and MPEG.

Afterward, we will look at common terms in multimedia.

> ***Reality Check*** *Throughout this section I will discuss audio and video. Keep in mind that sound (audio) can include music, sound effects, digitized voice, or simple tones. Video refers to any digitally encoded motion video that includes full-motion video and animation.*

What is JPEG?

The Joint Pictures Expert Group (JPEG) format supports high-resolution graphics and compression. Compression reduces the size of JPEG files. However, the higher the compression the more image data that is lost and the lower the quality. Related files end with the .jpg or .jpeg extension.

JPEG is only one of many available formats for images. Other popular formats for images include:

- **Bitmap** This file format is used with screen captures and other bitmapped files. Related files end with the .bmp extension.

- **GIF** The Graphics Interchange File (GIF) format is best used with low resolution to moderate resolution graphics as well as with graphics that have lots of text. Related files end with the .gif extension. By reducing the colors in the color palette and using options such as dithering, GIF images can be squeezed into smaller size files.

- **PNG** The Portable Network Graphics (PNG) format supports lossless compression ensuring images can be squeezed into smaller files without reducing quality. Related files end with the .png extension.

These graphic formats are the popular formats used on the World Wide Web. GIF is a good format to use with standard graphics or graphics containing text. JPEG is a good format to use for high-resolution graphics and pictures. PNG is a good format to use to squeeze high-quality graphics into smaller size files. The least efficient of these file formats is BMP. Typically BMP files are much larger than the same files converted to GIF, JPEG, or PNG.

What is MPEG?

A more correct question to ask would really be: Who is MPEG and what is MPEG? This is because MPEG refers to a group of people and a standard. The Moving Picture Expert Group (MPEG) is a group of people that meet to develop and discuss standards for digital video and audio compression.

The group is a subcommittee of the International Standards Organization (ISO). They meet several times a year to discuss the technical aspects of digital video and audio compression, and thus the MPEG standard is an industry standard for compressing and decompressing digital video and audio.

How Does MPEG Differ from

JPEG?

JPEG is a standard for still image compression and it is commonly used with digital images, such as photographs. MPEG is a standard for moving images and audio.

The key difference here is still (nonmoving) versus moving images. At first the notion of moving images versus still images may seem similar.

After all, moving pictures are just sequences of pictures changing in time. In actuality, when you add motion—changes in time—you end up with a completely different problem.

Sound and moving video fall under the same standard because both can change with time and can be defined by sequences in time. Since this is true, similar techniques can be used to deal with them.

The MPEG Standard

MPEG seeks to define standards for multimedia that will enable multimedia objects to be used on any computer system. True standards workable on any system are extremely important.

While the Moving Pictures Expert Group is striving to improve standards, a number of forces are working against them. Different computer manufacturers, such as Macintosh and IBM, have different techniques for displaying video and playing sound. Further, these techniques have been in use for years, making it very difficult to adopt a universal standard.

The good news is that, thanks to the MPEG subcommittee and

other subcommittees in the International Standards Organization, there are a few universal standards for sound and video. The standards also make it easier for software developers to develop multimedia tools that handle compression and decompression.

The MPEG standard is seeking to define several progressive levels, where each advance in level represents a significant advance in the technology required to meet the successive level.

What this means is the first level in MPEG was designed to set the standard for its time, the second level was designed to set the standard for its time and so on. In this way the MPEG standard will continue to evolve as technology evolves and will be something for industry leaders to strive to achieve.

Currently, there are two world standards in MPEG video—MPEG-1 and MPEG-2—and two standards in MPEG audio—MPEG 3 and MPEG 4. If you've seen live video played on a computer, you've probably seen what MPEG level 1 video looks like.

The relatively small picture was played at roughly 30 frames per second with audio quality comparable to an audio CD. There were some tricks that could be used to make the image larger, but the effective resolution was still 352x240 pixels.

In 1995, MPEG-2 became the high-quality standard in video. It offers true full-screen play capability at 640x480 pixels at 30 frames per second (US). MPEG-3 or MP3 as it is commonly called, has been widely used to produce CD-quality audio since around 1998 and has gained great popularity on the Internet.

Another popular format is the Advanced Audio Coding (AAC) format. AAC files are also referred to as MP4 files. Although MP3 is the audio format most everyone recognizes, AAC actually is nearly as widely used as AAC is the default format for the Apple iPod. AAC is one of several audio coding formats defined by the International Standards Organization (ISO) for MPEG. AAC was first specified as MPEG-2 AAC, and then enhanced and extended within MPEG-4. Apple's popular iTunes music service uses the AAC format.

AAC uses a perceptual coding technique to compress digital audio files. AAC is similar to MP3, but offers a number of advantages designed to improve audio quality, including higher-efficiency compression and better handling of audio frequencies above 16 kilohertz (kHz).

Millions of people have traded digital music files using MP3- and MP4-encoding. The improved efficiency of AAC files makes AAC a better choice than MP3 for some projects.

What Is MPEG Compression All About?

Just as JPEG images and other graphic images can be compressed, so can digital audio and video. While MPEG is a technical standard for compression, not a compression algorithm, manufacturers who follow the MPEG standard will develop or obtain a proprietary compression algorithm to achieve what the standard defines.

A compression algorithm is a programmed mathematical formula for squeezing audio and video into smaller disk spaces. Sound and video that takes up less disk space will require less network bandwidth and will also download faster.

Some compression algorithms are superior to others because they are more efficient in the way they squeeze the audio and video. More efficiency normally translates to better quality when the audio or video is decompressed, or unsqueezed, during playback. The emphasis here is on the word normally.

When compressing multimedia files, you generally select a compression ratio and a quality setting. A compression ratio is the ratio at which audio or video is compressed.

A general range that you can compress files in is from 2:1 to 100:1. The larger the compression ratio, the smaller the resulting file at a direct sacrifice to quality when later decompressed.

> **Reality Check** *A 20:1 (20-to-1) compression ratio, means the file will be squeezed into a space approximately 1/20th of its original size. When you are squeezing that much space out of original material something has to give, and normally it is the quality of the playback. An exception is MPEG-2 that can compress at 30:1 with no visible loss in image quality and can compress video up to 200:1.*

A quality setting is a largely arbitrary scale describing the tradeoff to make between the resulting size of the file and its quality during playback. A general range for quality setting is from 1 to 100.

The higher the quality setting the larger the resulting file will be and the better its quality. Quality settings often confuse people because a quality setting of 75 does not mean keeping 75% of the information. The compression ratio describes how much information to squeeze out of the file.

The quality setting is more of a reality check. Let's say you'd like to compress at a ratio of 50:1 but want a quality factor of 100. The file created after you compress with these settings will not be significantly smaller. If you use a rational setting like compression 7:1 and a quality factor of 75, the result will be much smaller files and higher quality playback.

If the concept of compressing files seems confusing, do not get frustrated. Compression algorithms are complex beasts. Let someone else worry about the inner workings of compression algorithms.

The bottom line about MPEG compression algorithms is: They are highly effective in squeezing the size of our audio and video files, and this makes it easy to use them in presentations and digital publications.

Considerations to Make Before Adding Multimedia

Understanding basic multimedia concepts is extremely important. Now that you know what multimedia is, you can make an informed decision before adding multimedia to your work.

Multimedia will put more demands on your system and on the system you use to deliver the finished product to viewers. You should check the location where you'll be delivering the presentation to ensure that the multimedia will be effective.

In the boardroom or classroom, you may need additional equipment, such as speakers, to ensure members of the audience can hear sounds or you may need a large screen television to deliver your video component.

You should include multimedia to enhance the work, not to distract. Each and every bit of sound, whether music, speech, or simple tones, should serve a purpose. The same goes when you add video. The key to using multimedia is to minimize information overload while maximizing value.

Overwhelm the viewer with gizmos and sound effects that do not serve a useful purpose and your production will fail. Use multimedia in moderation. The most effective multimedia is simple in its design.

Your use of multimedia also may be limited by the work's:

- **Audience**
- **Purpose**
- **Scope**

Select multimedia that is appropriate for a particular project's audience and purpose. Limit the amount of multimedia in the project according to the scope of the project.

The reasons for including multimedia do not have to be lofty; rather they should tie-in with the purpose of the project.

Let's Talk Sound

Sound can be a powerful medium to get your message across. When incorporating sound into your work, you should always follow a few simple rules:

- Sound should never be distracting.

- Sound should serve a useful purpose, even if only to entertain.
- You should be able to turn the sound off and on, as well as to restart the sound as necessary—even in the lecture hall.
- In the case of music, it should tie in with the theme of the presentation or work.

Keep in mind that sound adds a new dimension to any work. To play sound, most computers require a special sound card. To play sound in a conference room or meeting hall, you may need special equipment, such as a hi-fi stereo system and speakers.

Different operating systems have different and very often incompatible sound formats. We will look at sound formats in a moment. For now, let's explore the types of sound and how they can be used:

Music

Sound effects

Digitized voice

Music

Music is a great type of sound to include in your work and your presentations. The type of music you can use includes:

- Traditional compositions
- The latest single from a compact disk
- Original music scores composed on a computer

If you are a musician at heart, you could easily use software tools available today to create spectacular compositions. But not everyone (me for one) is musically inclined.

Most musical compositions, especially original computer compositions and any commercially recorded music on CD-ROM, belong to the owner of the music. Before using this type of music in a public forum, you may need to get written permission or pay a fee.

Brevity in the music you use is an important point. Use it as an introduction, a way to get the audience's attention or break the ice, but then turn it off!

Sound Effects

Sound effects are fun because they are often easy types of sound to create. With a microphone and the plain-jane sound recording tool that came with your computer you can digitize your own sound effects.

For example, PC sound boards normally include a microphone jack and a sound recording tool, so all you have to do is plug in the microphone, and you are ready to create sound effects of anything and everything from the dog barking, the kids screaming, or the wind in the palms.

The sound of a dog barking will not be appropriate for most work, but could be just the comic relief needed when presenting the storyboards for a children's story. The sound of a creaking door could be great in a murder mystery just before the denouement.

As with music, use sound effects for a specific reason, be brief and use the effects sparingly. Less is more in this case.

Digitized Voice

Digitized voice can be useful. If you've used America Online before, you've seen a practical way to include brief digitized voice messages.

Basically, the America Online program says, "Welcome," when you start the program and has additional short greetings or sayings when you enter or leave other key places, such as, "You have mail."

These verbal cues serve a useful purpose and primarily call your attention to something.

After a time though, verbal cues can become annoying, so again, less is more. Remember, even the most pleasant things can become annoying.

Sound Formats

Concerning audio, there are many formats that are so popular they seem to be industry standards. Sun Microsystem's AU format was once very popular, but its popularity did not stem from the playback quality of AU recordings, which is very poor. It was so popular because it could be used on any computer system.

Things in the audio world change quickly and today's formats may not be tomorrow's. Excellent pure sample formats are AIFF for Macintosh and WAV for Microsoft Windows. Although these two formats are very popular on their respective systems, you may not be able to play them on different operating systems without conversion.

The key thing to note is that if your presentation or work includes sound, you should ensure that you know what operating system the presentation computer will be using and whether the computer supports the sound format you are using.

Don't fly off to that meeting without all the audio/video equipment you need to get the job done—even if the only equipment needed is a laptop. You may be surprised to find that the loaner laptop you get is still running Windows 2000 and doesn't support the audio format you are using.

Bit Rates and Sampling Frequencies

Whenever you work with sound, you'll want to look closely at the bit rate and sampling frequency. With bits rates, the higher the bit rate, the higher the audio quality and the larger the file size. Bit rates on the low end of the scale are suitable for voice-only recordings, such as spoken-word audio books while higher bits rates are better suited to music. For example, a bit rate of 128 kilobits-per-second (kbps) provides fair quality for music while a bit rate of 192 kbps provides good quality for music.

The sampling frequency determines the number of times per second the audio waveforms are captured digitally. The higher the sampling frequency, the higher the quality and the larger the file size. A sampling frequency of 44.1 kHz provides CD quality audio. A sampling frequency of 48.0 kHz provides studio quality audio.

With MP3, a 60-minute audio CD encoded at 128 kbps uses about 57 MB while the same CD encoded at 192 kbps uses about 86 MB. When converting audio, don't choose a bit rate or sampling frequency that is higher than the bit rate or sampling frequency used to store the audio originally. You'll waste space and won't get fidelity improvements.

Let's Talk Video

Video is another powerful medium to get your message across. Playing digitized video on your computer is a fairly recent actuality, which is good news and bad news.

To display video, most computer users will need a video card or some type of special equipment. If that video is intended to be displayed on a projection screen using a projector, the projector display settings and allowable video modes will have a great impact on the ability to view the video (as well as the quality of the video).

When you work with video, you should keep in mind the two key broadcast standards. NTSC is the broadcast standard in North America and Japan. PAL is the broadcast standard for most of Europe. Switching between these formats can cause problems and don't expect to be able to play your NTSC video everywhere in the world.

> ***Reality Check*** *Programs are available that let you display digitized PAL on an NTSC monitor and vice versa. What this means to you is that if your video is viewable only on an NTSC monitor/projector and you need to be able to display the video on a PAL monitor/project, you will want to obtain a NTSC-PAL converter program.*

Let's explore the two basic types of video:

- **Animation**
- **Motion Video**

Animation

You have only to watch the latest blockbuster movie or watch Saturday morning cartoons to see that computerized animation is big business. Computer animation can also be a good technique for presentation and digital media.

The idea of animation is conceptually very simple. You draw a number of individual still images and play them back in a series as if they were a film.

For example, to bounce a ball inside a box, you could draw a consecutive series of images, moving the ball slightly in each new image. When played back, the slight variances in the location of the ball will make the ball seem to move around the inside the box.

To fit in with your work, animation has to seem a part of the work. This may sound redundant, but accept it at face value for a moment.

If your work is an interactive role-playing game where the main character or characters can be maneuvered around the screen, the animation of the character would seem a natural part of the work. If your work is a Web site directed at young adults or children, a similarly animated character could turn the pages for readers. This would also seem a natural part of the work.

On the other hand, if the work is the digital version of the Communications of the ACM (Association for Computing

Machinery), this animated character would not have a natural place in the work.

Motion Video

The digitizing of "live" video has great potential and will continue to be a growth area for years to come. The applications for live video in presentations, interactive multimedia, and digital media are limited only by your imagination. Generally, live video works best as the featured component or as a way to get the viewer/reader's attention.

If you elect to use video, keep in mind that times are changing. The idea of digitized video in creative works is not so new anymore and the world that once accepted poor quality because it had no substitutes has evolved.

Today, even in the corporate meeting room, people expect to see polished video work or to not see video at all. Pay close attention to the quality of the product—those viewing the video certainly will.

Video Formats

The most widely used video format is MPEG, the industry standard. This is a pleasant change from the audio side of the house. As the standard, MPEG video can be played on any computer system.

Apple's QuickTime format is not far behind MPEG in popularity. QuickTime is gaining popularity so rapidly in large part due to Apple's excellent support for the format and its promotion.

A QuickTime player is included in Apple's operating systems and available freely for other operating systems. QuickTime has good audio track features and good playback quality.

Microsoft's Video for Windows format, AVI, is another popular format. While it was once the dominating format for the Microsoft Windows environment, its usage is decreasing in favor of MPEG and QuickTime.

Let's Talk New Media

In the ever-expanding, ever-changing world of multimedia two newer technologies that you have to acquaint yourself with are:

- E-Ink
- **Electronic Paper Displays**

E-Ink

E-ink technology is what makes reading on Amazon Kindle Sony Reader similar to reading text on paper. The high-contrast, high-resolution displays on these readers make them readable in direct sunlight and at angles up to 180 degrees. When you turn pages in an electronic book (e-book), these readers use power to turn on the e-ink pixels. Once a page is displayed, these readers don't use power to maintain the page. This helps ensure the battery lasts longer than a standard Portable Digital Assistant (PDA).

E-ink contains millions of tiny microcapsules, about the diameter of a human hair. In one version of the technology, each microcapsule contains positively charged white particles and negatively charged black particles suspended in a clear fluid. When a positive electric field is applied, the black particles move to the top of the microcapsule where they become visible to the user and this is what makes the surface appear black at that spot. Simultaneously, an opposite electric field pulls the white particles to the bottom of the microcapsules where they are hidden from view. By reversing this process, the white particles appear at the top of the capsule, which makes the surface appear white at that spot.

Electronic Paper Displays

To create an Electronic Paper Display (EPD) for an electronic device, e-ink is printed onto a sheet of plastic film. By laminating this film to a layer of circuitry, the circuitry forms a pattern of pixels that can then be controlled by a display driver. The screen printing process can be used to create an EPD on virtually any surface, including glass, plastic, fabric and even paper.

One of the first EPDs was demonstrated by Lucent and E Ink Corporation in November 2000. This display was an early prototype that used flexible transistors. By June 2002, E Ink Corporation developed a 2mm thick flexible active-matrix display on steel foil transistor substrates. In December 2004, Plastic Logic and E Ink Corporation unveiled a flexible all-plastic display. This was the first EPD display that truly was suitable for use with electronic devices.

Many EPD variants are available, including segmented displays and active matrix displays. Segmented displays are low-power, low-performance displays that can be used to convey basic information using letters, numbers, and pre-defined icons. As the name implies, segmented displays are divided into discrete segments that can be controlled individually and attached to a surface, such as a shelf display or a mini MP3 player. Active matrix displays are high-resolution, high-performance displays that are designed to be used with electronic devices.

EPDs with black and white particles and active matrix displays are able to reproduce the feel of printed books, newspapers and magazines. They offer true black and true white as well as gradients of black and white referred to as grayscale. Early EPDs support 4 grayscale levels (also referred to as 2-bit grayscale). This means they effectively display black, dark gray, medium gray, and white.

Newer EPDs with black and white particles support higher grayscale levels for richer, more dynamic viewing experiences. With 3-bit grayscale, an EPD supports eight grayscale levels, allowing for six gradients of gray between black and white. With 4-bit grayscale, an EPD supports sixteen grayscale levels, allowing for fourteen gradients of gray between black and white. Generally, the resolution of these displays is at least 170 pixels per inch or higher.

EPDs with color particles are becoming available. E Ink Corporation and Toppan Printing Co. Ltd. demonstrated a color EPD in October 2005. This display supports 12-bit color with a resolution of 83 pixels per inch. By using microcapsules that combine red, green, blue, and white particles, the display preserves the paper-like whiteness of a printed page while enabling rich blacks for text and a range of colors and tones for images. The color particles also are used to smooth black and white text for enhanced legibility. EPDs with color particles need to achieve higher resolutions and lower production costs to be practical for reader devices.

Sony Reader and Amazon Kindle

Sony unveiled its first reader device in January 2006 and the device became available in early 2007. Amazon unveiled its first reader in early 2008.

The Sony Reader and the Amazon Kindle both have a black-and-white active matrix display. Like E Ink itself, these readers have evolved through several generations of products. The original Sony Reader and the original Amazon Kindle supported 4 grayscale levels and were able to switch the display at a typical rate of 1.2 seconds. This meant that the device typically displayed the next page in an e-book in 1.2 seconds.

Newer reader models including Sony PRS-505, Sony PRS-700 and Kindle 2 support 8 grayscale levels or higher and are able to more rapidly switch the display. The typical display switch rate is 40% faster than the original reader at .74 seconds or less. This means that the device typically displays the next page in an e-book in .74 seconds or less. Additionally, as the PRS-700 has a faster processor than the PRS-505, the PRS-700 is able to more quickly render the page for the display.

If your work will be available on reader devices, you'll want to ensure you create separate versions of your work that are optimized for reader devices. The Sony Reader and the Amazon Kindle both have a 6-inch screen that provides a resolution of 600x800 pixels—or approximately 170 pixels per inch. This display resolution is in stark contrast to display resolutions used on desktop and laptop computers which have screen resolutions ranging from 800x600 on the low end to 1920x1200 on the high end. It also should be noted that while screens on readers are taller than they are wide, screens on computers are wider than they are tall.

The Critical Question Of Resources

The problem with multimedia is that you can quickly become caught up in the vortex of technology. With multimedia, for every level of technology you advance, you increase complexity and the margin for error. At some point, you have to ask yourself:

- Is this going as expected?
- Is it time to bring in outside help?
- Is it time to drop the multimedia aspects entirely?

The answers to these questions don't have to be all or nothing. Sometimes, you'll want to bring in some temporary help to give the work that extra bit of multimedia polish that's needed while dropping plans for other multimedia components.

Before making a hasty decision, you may want to go back to the reasons you decided to use multimedia in the first place and reevaluate the project and your goals.

Part III: Quick Review

Adding multimedia—graphics, sound and video—to your work is not only a possibility today, it is often required. Charts, graphs, and images add pizzazz to your work. Sound and video can significantly enhance any publicly presented works. The key to using multimedia is to minimize information overload while maximizing value.

While consumers crave multimedia, you should take into account many considerations before adding sound or video to your publication. You should carefully consider the purpose of the multimedia, audience, project scope and hardware requirements.

Before you continue, try the following exercise:

Exercise

Continuing the previous assignments, replace the graphic placeholders with actual artwork or photographs in the previously created documents. Resize the graphics as necessary. You can use any existing artwork or pictures. These don't have to be in the same theme as the assignment.

After you add the graphics, optimize the layout for the actual size of the images you are using and then try printing the sample documents. If you have trouble adding the graphics, size and print the graphics separately and then use the old-fashioned cut and paste method to add the pictures to the printed document.

You can also cut out the text and then try rearranging the text and the pictures on a blank piece of paper to achieve the best layout.

Part IV: Delivering Your Work

You have written an essay, novel, report, presentation or other creative work. The document resides on your computer's hard drive, waiting to go out into the world.

Getting to this stage in the writing process has taken many days or weeks. The urge to submit the finished work is almost overpowering, but a voice in the back of your mind keeps you from whisking it out to the world.

Guess what? You should listen to the voice.

This section explores the steps you should take to proof your work. You will learn

- What to look for when proofing
- Tips for spell checking the publication
- Tips for grammar checking the publication
- How to catch typos outside the main text
- How to catch inconsistencies
- How to balance the need for perfection with efficiency and timeliness

Chapter 13: Last Minute Gotchas

You have not worked this hard to fail simply because you did not proof the work. Ensuring the quality of the work will take only a few hours.

That is a small price to pay to ensure the work is the best it can be, especially considering you might have spent hundreds of hours writing and creating the work.

Producing a high-quality product will also help you build credibility. Your credibility as a student, worker or freelancer is the key to your success.

What to Look For when Proofing

When you proof something, you are checking the final copy to ensure it is error-free (or as error-free as possible). In the old days, proofing meant there was an ominous stack of freshly typed pages sitting on your desktop.

The thicker the stack of pages, the more ominous the proofing process seemed. You hunkered down over your desk with a dozen red pens and toiled for countless hours.

A few days or weeks later those pages no longer looked fresh. They were splattered with red ink from end to end—a dozen or more different proofing symbols you scratched onto the pages.

If you were fortunate enough to be an editor, you could send the work back to the writer. If you were both editor and writer, you dusted off the typewriter and went to work.

Today, many creative projects will never see the printed page before they are delivered in finished form. The easily manipulated form of a project in a word processing file make it all too easy to revise online. This is fine most of the time.

There is no point in wasting paper printing a work that will never be seen in printed form. However, in the age of the computerized spelling and grammar checkers, some people even neglect to read their own words for accuracy and consistency.

Their editing and proofing process consists entirely of two steps: spell checking and grammar checking. They rely on the spell checker to find their typos and on the grammar checker to catch the remaining mistakes.

Good writers know that no matter what percentage of the errors spelling and grammar checkers claim to find, the critical mistakes will be found only through careful proofing.

For example, your spelling checker will not find any of the errors in the following sentences:

- The whether outside was sunny and did not altar our plans.
- He wade each claws and decided three were knot kneaded.
- Who wood have guest what he mite dew.
- Not being able to urn a wage is know miner issue.

My spell checker went through those sentences in less than a second and reported no errors at all. This is because spell checkers do not care if you use the wrong words. They only check for valid words. If a word is valid, they will pass it by.

I decided it might be fun to run the same sentences through

my grammar checker. After all, it claims to find 97 percent of the errors I will ever make.

Following the advice of the grammar checker, I blindly revised. Each time the grammar checker made a suggestion, I followed it.

Here is how the revision progressed, until the grammar checker claimed the paragraph had no errors:

Sentence 1

- **Original**: The whether outside was sunny and did not altar our plans.
- **Revised**: Whether outside was sunny and did not altar our plans.
- **Revised**: Whether outside was sunny, did not altar our plans.
- **Final**: Whether outside was sunny, did not alter our plans.

Sentence 2

- **Original**: He wade each claws and decided three were knot kneaded.
- **Revised**: He wade each claw and decided three were knot kneaded.
- **Revised**: He wades each claw and decided three were knot kneaded.
- **Revised**: He waded each claw and decided three were knot kneaded.
- **Final**: He waded each claw and decided three were not kneaded.

Sentence 3

- **Original**: Who wood have guest what he mite dew.
- **Revised**: Who wood have guested what he mite dew.
- **Revised**: Who woods have guested what he mite dew.
- **Final**: Whom woods have guested what he mite dew.

Sentence 4

- **Original**: Not being able to urn a wage is know miner issue.
- **Revised**: Not could urn a wage is know miner issue.
- **Final**: Not could earn a wage is know miner issue.

Although the results are comical, the truth is not. Grammar checkers follow rules outlined in their programming. The suggestions they offer are also in the programming.

Unless someone produces an artificially intelligent grammar-checking program, computer software will not replace the human mind for its ability to reliably check the written word.

Use spelling and grammar checkers to find the tedious errors; the typos or grammar mistakes you made because you were tired, didn't want to break the creative process by reaching for the dictionary, or otherwise.

Even though the critical mistakes are up to you to find, you do not have to do so blindly. There are many tips for finding spelling and grammar errors that will save you time and frustration.

Tips for Checking Spelling

Some books on the subject of writing and editing stress the importance of learning the correct spelling of words. They provide dozens of tips and tricks for remembering the spelling of words, stating rules like "i before e except after c." They provide long lists of commonly misspelled words and advise you to watch out for them.

Although spelling is important, it is not so important that it should keep you from creating anything.

To find the common mistakes use a spelling checker. A spelling checker may also be able to help you find inconsistently spelled technical terms. Most word processors include a spelling checker.

Remember, the accuracy of the spelling will only be as good as the checker's database of words.

Some spelling checkers boast 80,000 to 100,000 word dictionaries. Others have relatively few words. If your spelling checker does not recognize a word, you should consult a dictionary.

> **Reality Check** *The best dictionary for any serious writer is an unabridged dictionary. If a spelling checker that has a dictionary of 80,000 or more words is telling you it does not recognize a word, you*

may need the expanded word base of an unabridged dictionary. You can find print versions and digital versions of unabridged dictionaries.

Unabridged dictionaries often contain a wealth of resources. For example, Webster's Encyclopedic Unabridged Dictionary of the English Language, *distributed by Crown Publishing Group, is a one-stop resource for spelling and grammar. In addition to over 250,000 words, it contains:*

- An atlas of the world
- A brief chronology of history
- Important U.S. data from the Constitution to the Declaration of Independence
- A manual of style; rules for grammar
- A bad speller's dictionary
- An abbreviated French-English and English-French dictionary
- An abbreviated German-English and English-German dictionary
- An abbreviated Italian-English and English-Italian dictionary
- An abbreviated Spanish-English and English-Spanish dictionary
- A crossword puzzle dictionary

After the spelling checker has completed the chore of cleaning up most of the text, you should proof the text and look for incorrect word usage. The primary source of incorrect words will come from words that look alike or sound alike but have different meanings.

A grammar checker will catch the commonly confused words if they are used improperly in a sentence. However, if the word seems to be used properly in the sentence, a grammar checker will not find the incorrect word.

Studies have shown that certain words cause more confusion than others. The common ones like set/sit and lay/lie a grammar checker will usually catch.

The grammar checker finds errors associated with these words by looking mostly for direct or indirect objects that should accompany these words.

Here is a list of commonly confused words that your grammar checker might not catch:

Accede	Exceed	
Accept	Except	
Access	Excess	
Adept	Adopt	
Advice	Advise	
Affect	Effect	
Affluent	Effluent	
Attributed	Contributed	
Block	Bloc	
Cite	Sight	Site
Complement	Compliment	
Compose	Comprise	
Confuse	Complicate	
Demolish	Destroy	

Describe	Prescribe	
Discreet	Discrete	
Elicit	Illicit	
Eminent	Immanent	Imminent
Faze	Phase	
Fliers	Flyers	
Flout	Flaunt	
Forward	Foreword	
Imply	Infer	
Leave	Let	
Marshall	Marshal	
Mean	Average	Median
Moral	Morale	
Peddle	Pedal	
Personal	Personnel	
Precede	Proceed	
Principal	Principle	
Quiet	Quite	
Regulate	Relegate	
Residence	Residents	
Respectfully	Respectively	
Role	Roll	
Stationary	Stationery	
Whether	Weather	

A good resource to consult for incorrect words is a bad speller's dictionary. The typical bad speller's dictionary will have lists of look-alikes and sound-alikes. Lists will contain pairs of words that can be quickly searched.

Each word in the list will have a brief description. Usually, the description is one or two words, which makes the dictionary small and easy to search. For example:

Exercise: practice spirits

Exorcise: drive away evil

Veracity: truth

Voracity: hunger

Tips for Checking Grammar

The English language is one of the most difficult languages on the planet. It is no surprise that English grammar is the most troublesome area of writing.

When you write, you have to worry about subject and verb agreement, predicates, punctuation, and more.

If you spend too much time worrying about grammar, you probably will get writer's block. As you write, you should concentrate on the creative processes and not editing and proofing processes.

To find the common mistakes use a grammar checker. The best word processors include grammar checkers, but you might have to purchase one separately.

Remember, grammar checkers are only as good as the rules they use as the basis for the checking.

You can usually follow rule templates based on the style of writing you are working on, such as fiction, nonfiction, or technical. A grammar template for a fiction work will have a set of rules that normally apply to fiction writing.

Grammar checkers will let you customize the rules any way you want. You can turn off rules permanently or only for the session you are currently working on. The more rules you turn off, the lower the efficiency of the check. If you turn off too many rules the grammar checker will be useless.

Usually, it is best to follow the grammar templates set up by the experts who created the software. This means if you are working on a general nonfiction work, select the grammar template that applies to general nonfiction.

> **Reality Check** *Good resources to consult for grammar questions are style manuals. Styles manuals are the best sources to turn to for grammar, capitalization and punctuation issues.* The Little Brown Book *by Little Brown and Company is a comprehensive English grammar reference. For technical works, the* Publication Manual of the American Psychological Association *is terrific. The* MLA Handbook for Writers of Research Papers *is another good reference.*
>
> *Styles manuals are also the best sources to turn to for formatting questions. They can answer your questions pertaining to the use of lists, tables, figures, footnotes, equations, and citations. My personal preference out of the many style manuals available is the APA manual mentioned above. The APA manual spells out every point about format clearly and in great detail.*

After the grammar checker has found most of your mistakes, follow through by carefully reading your work. The biggest problem areas are

- Determining the proper case
- Subject-verb agreement
- Noun-pronoun agreement
- Dangling modifiers
- Predicates

The sections that follow examine each of these potential problem areas.

Determining the Proper Case

Determining the proper case for pronouns is a common problem area. The *case* of a word refers to the way the word is used in a sentence.

There are four cases:

Nominative   *Nominative* pronouns are the subject of a clause.

Possessive   *Possessive* pronouns show who or what something belongs to.

Objective   *Objective* pronouns are objects of verbs or prepositions.

Reflexive   *Reflexive* pronouns refer to a noun or pronoun that has already appeared in the sentence.

Table 1 shows the proper singular and plural cases for pronouns.

Table 1: Singular and plural pronouns

Nominative Pronouns	Singular
	I, you, he, she, it, one, who
	Plural
	We, you, they
Possessive Pronouns	Singular
	my/mine, your/yours, his, her/hers, its, one's, whose
	Plural
	our/ours, your/yours, their/theirs
Objective Pronouns	Singular
	me, you, him, her, it, one, whom
	Plural
	us, you, them
Reflexive Pronouns	Singular
	myself, yourself, himself, herself, itself, oneself
	Plural
	ourselves, yourselves, themselves

Subject-Verb Agreement

Subjects and verbs agree when they are both singular or both plural. Most problems occur when the subject and verb are separated in the sentence. This separation of the subject and verb even causes problems for grammar checkers, which often assume the subject is the noun that occurs immediately before the verb.

For example:

> **Incorrect**: The children who went to the circus was laughing and playing.
>
> **Correct**: The children who went to the circus were laughing and playing.

When proofing, match the subject and verb of each sentence about which you have a question. Sometimes it is easier to reword the sentence so the subject and verb are closer together.

Noun-Pronoun Agreement

Nouns and pronouns agree when the pronoun is the same person or number as the noun to which it refers. This means singular pronouns should be used with singular nouns and plural pronouns should be used with plural nouns.

The pronoun should be in the same person as the noun when appropriate. Each pronoun should also refer to a specific noun. If it does not, add a noun to correct the problem.

For example:

> **Incorrect**: The captain asked yourself where he had gone wrong.
>
> **Correct**: The captain asked himself where he had gone wrong.

Dangling Modifiers

Words or phrases that give more information about the subject, verb, or object of a clause are *modifiers*. A dangling modifier occurs when there is nothing to give more information about because the subject, verb, or object is not in the sentence.

This problem occurs most often in sentences beginning with a verb that ends in -ing because the modifier must modify the subject of the sentence.

If you have a question about whether a sentence has a dangling modifier, rewrite it. You might find that when you rework the sentence you will add in the modifier if it was missing from the original sentence. For example:

Incorrect: Walking home, the truck went up the hill.

Correct: As I walked home, I saw the truck go up the hill.

Predicates

Every sentence contains two basic parts: a subject and a predicate. A *predicate* consists of a verb and all the words modifying or attributed to the verb. These modifying words or attributes are called the *compliment*.

The predicate usually states the action performed by the subject or the status of the subject. The verb should describe the action done by or done to the subject.

For example:

Incorrect: The book set down on the table.

Correct: The book is on the table.

Correct: John set the book down on the table.

How to Catch Typos Outside Main Text

When you are proofing the project, you are looking primarily at the main text areas. An area of the project that is easily overlooked is the text that occurs outside the main text, such as in graphs and charts. This text also needs to be checked for typos.

Headings on pages contain text. Images often include captions. This text is easily neglected because you are so familiar with it. After all, you created it and added it to the pages. This means you will have to check the unique text on every page.

Proofreading for typos is hard because people tend to see what should be there and not what is really there. To catch typos that you might have been staring at and not noticed for weeks as you developed the work, you should look at the work in a new way.

One way to force yourself to look at the actual text instead of what you believe is there is to go through the work backward. Start on the last page and work toward the front page.

Remember, you will only have to read unique textual components that are not a part of the main text you should have already checked. If you used a master page, the task will be much easier than if you did not.

This is because you will only have to check a few unique pages or unique features of an individual page. When you check the master page, read the text slowly. Sometimes it helps to read each individual word backward letter by letter. This will help you see the actual word.

Another tip is that if you find a typo on a page, do not relax and think the odds are slim that you will find another typo on the same page. On any page where you find a typo, you should reread the page at least once, and possibly twice. This will ensure you do not miss a typo close to the first typo.

Finally, do not forget to check images, figures, or charts. Text included as part of graphics is easy to neglect, especially if you have to select a print option to view the image. You should do this even for images you believe do not contain text. You might be surprised to find text and greatly relieved when you find and fix a typo you otherwise would have missed.

How to Catch Inconsistencies

When you are reviewing, it is easy to miss inconsistencies. After all, you are looking at macrostructure, which may include material you haven't already proofed, such as footnotes, reference pages and table of contents. This is why it is easy to miss inconsistencies in the work.

To find something you must first look for it.

Inconsistencies are easily missed because you are so familiar with the core work that you don't critically examine additional materials or the macrostructure of the work. You created every page of the work and should know it better than anyone else.

An example of an inconsistency is a heading that tells the reader this is Chapter 4 while the main text is from Chapter 3. Unless the text for every chapter begins with a chapter number, this inconsistency is easily missed.

To check for this type of inconsistency do one of the following:

- Separate supplementary pages from the main text and proof them separately.
- Check chapter numbers in headers and chapter numbers in text references to be sure they are correct.
- Double-check table of contents, footnote and index references to make sure they are accurate.
- Check the chapter order to make sure the actual structure is what you think it is.

To check for inconsistencies you might have to check hundreds of pages. For example, a duplicate page is often easy to find. However, a missing page is often difficult to notice.

To check for missing or duplicate pages do one of the following:

- If you included pages numbers, make sure the numbers are sequential in the final document. Investigate any out of order numbering or missing numbers.
- If the numbering skips, you should first check the page numbering feature of your word processor or presentation software. You may have started numbering of a new section or file incorrectly.

The placement of charts, graphs and other graphics can also create an inconsistent look in the work. To check for misplaced items, you should print out the work or use the print preview feature of the software application you are using.

When you use multiple fonts, you can also create inadvertent inconsistencies. Changes in font size can be subtle, but changes in font type should be obvious.

Look for inconsistencies in any unique items you added to individual pages, especially when you added components late in the development process. You might have changed fonts when you were working on other parts of the project.

A quick check to ensure the fonts are consistent throughout the work is a good precaution.

Balancing Perfection with Efficiency and Timeliness

Creating a finished work that has no typos, inconsistencies, or other errors would be a wonderful thing, but in the real world less-than-perfect products are released every day. At some point, you have to ask:

- How much proofing is enough?
- How many typos are too many—a hundred, a dozen, less?
- How much testing is enough?
- How many inconsistencies are too many—10, one, or none?
- When do you stop?
- When should you stop?

The answers are not easy. Every day a writer somewhere is making these decisions based on balancing the need for perfection with efficiency and timeliness.

Because of their size, some mediums are easier to check for accuracy. A short work, such as a 20-page report, is much easier to proof than a 300-page book. Yet reports often contain typos, inconsistencies, and errors.

The real determinant for a project has little to do with size and more to do with timeliness. A monthly magazine must be published monthly. A weekly newsletter must be published weekly. A newspaper must be published every day and in some metropolitan areas twice a day—a morning and an evening edition.

At some point, a manager or editor has to make the decision to tell the writers to print what they have.

Time is also a major factor for publishing books. Some books have to go to the presses in three months to beat the competition. Other books have to go to the presses now or never to tie-in with a current event.

Look at the number of books rushed to the press for recent media events. Those books will sell today, but they will not sell in three months when the courtrooms clear.

In the end, your decision might also come down to money. Publishers cannot go on to other moneymaking projects while they are working full-time on something else. A finished work cannot make money unless it is for sale.

You should stop proofing and testing when it makes sense.

Base the decision on your needs and the need for perfection in the final product. If necessary, use time and money constraints to help you make the decision to continue checking the work or to stop.

Part IV: Quick Review

Good writers know that the critical mistakes will be found only through careful proofing. When you proof check your work, you look primarily at the main text areas. However, you should also check text that occurs outside the main text.

To make the proofing process manageable no matter the size and organization of the project, the process can be broken down into several parts. When you are proofing, it is easy to miss inconsistencies. To find inconsistencies, you must look for them.

Before you call it a day, try the following exercise:

Exercise

Continuing the previous assignments, use the techniques discussed in this section to check the documents you've created:

- Check spelling and grammar

- Proofread the documents

- Check graphics for typos and inconsistencies

- Double-check additional documents, like the title page and table of contents

About the Author

William Stanek is a leading technology expert and an award-winning author. Over the years, his practical advice has helped readers all over the world. He has written more than 100 books, which are sold all over the world and have been translated in many languages.

William is proud to have served in the Persian Gulf War. During the war, he flew numerous combat and combat support missions, logging over two hundred combat flight hours. His distinguished accomplishments during the Persian Gulf War earned him nine medals, including the United States of America's highest flying honor, the Air Force Distinguished Flying Cross.

Currently, William resides in the Pacific Northwest with his wife and children.

We Need You

Reagent Press is a small publisher. Without the help of you the reader, we will not be able to produce future works. If you liked the book, please tell your friends and associates! Thank you for your continued support!

www.ingramcontent.com/pod-product-compliance
Lightning Source LLC
Chambersburg PA
CBHW052051070526
44584CB00017B/2135